TREASURY OF
BIBLE STORIES

DONNA JO NAPOLI

ILLUSTRATIONS BY **CHRISTINA BALIT**

NATIONAL GEOGRAPHIC

WASHINGTON, D.C.

TABLE OF CONTENTS

Page 1: Doves are among the world's most common birds. This dove carries a sprig from the olive, an evergreen original to the Mediterranean area and famous for its oil and fruit.

Previous: Wells were an important source of freshwater for people and livestock, especially in rural communities. Here a family is gathered around one.

Note: Books of the Bible appear in bold.

INTRODUCTION

The stories in this book are my own reimaginings and retellings from the ancient Bible, often referred to as the Hebrew Bible by Jewish scholars and as the Old Testament by Christian scholars. These retellings are as faithful to the originals as I could manage with the weekly help of my guide, Rabbi Helen Plotkin, over the better part of a year. The stories include much beloved ones as well as some that may not be so commonly shared, but that are offered here in hopes of giving a fuller, more cohesive book overall. This volume carries us from the opening of the Book of Genesis to the end of the Book of Daniel. As such, the stories present a view of human history from the creation to the building of the second temple in Jerusalem.

Readers may be surprised at the very outset to find two creation stories, but this is true to the ancient Bible. In fact, in the ancient Bible several stories are told twice and these doublets often differ profoundly on matters of substance. Sometimes I have chosen to present both versions, particularly if they shed light on the nature of the divine (as with the creation stories). Other times I have blended versions (as with King David coming to know Saul). Still other times I offer only one version. The choice is based on what, in my eyes, makes the best overall book.

Readers may also be surprised to find two names for the divine—*God* and *Lord*—with distinct behaviors at the outset. These names are present in the original text (along with other names that are not pertinent to the stories offered here): *Elohim* (אלהים) for *God* and *Adonai* (a euphemism for the unpronounceable four-letter name יהוה) for *the Lord.* These name differences are present in all the common English translations, but they are often overlooked. Especially in the early stories, the different names seem to be linked to different aspects of the divine's character, a factor I have worked to make clear. Though both names continue to be used throughout the ancient Bible, the clarity of that distinction

is less obvious to me in the later stories (though biblical scholars still study this matter). Nevertheless, I call the divine by the name used in the ancient Bible in each story, so that the reader can have the benefit of the original.

The stories are not always ordered in a way that makes sense chronologically. For example, in the ancient Bible the story of Esther saving her people precedes the story of Daniel in the lions' den, even though Esther lives three generations after Daniel. Certainly there is some correlation to historical events in some stories; at times a story's chronology may match historical chronology quite well (such as the story of King David). But other times the chronology is confused. This confusion may reflect the fact that stories that might have originated true to historical chronology were passed down orally as cultural treasures rather than as historical accounts. Still other events are clearly metaphorical, with a sense that the beliefs they espouse reflect a divine plan rather than reflecting a strict history. Readers shouldn't be dismayed. The point is not to reason a straight path through the stories, but to wander about through them, perhaps knocking into the same plot lines multiple times, letting each encounter add another layer of meaning. The stories express ideological beliefs. They are founded in the faith that there is sense in the passing of time—shape and purpose to it that humans may find difficult to discern but that is surely there.

Like ancient stories in other cultures, we see here huge questions to wrestle with: How and why did life begin? What is our job, our purpose, during our time in this life? Does death (help to) give meaning to life? Will life on Earth go on forever or is there some ending point ahead? In other words, as the philosophers say: What's it all about?

The stories aim to give answers largely via interactions between humankind and the divine, and, sometimes, via interactions among

humans. We find no tidy, comfortable answers, however. Instead, we find insistence on harsh realities. Faith and loyalty are rewarded, but not always. Kindness and generosity are prized, but only usually. Trickery sometimes ends in success, but generally at a cost. Jealousy almost always bites its own tail, as does greed. Violence, particularly as a reaction to violence, is sometimes inevitable. No pretty picture is painted, possibly because it would be dangerous to do so. The people listening to or reading these ancient stories needed to understand what they were up against, or else they might be left unprepared and defenseless.

We see a world in which living beings experience great hardships. Survival is an ever-present issue, short-term and long-term. So much depends upon fertility. A woman's social status correlates positively with her ability to bear children, particularly sons. A barren woman is at the bottom. So much depends upon water. If the rains don't come, the crops and wells dry up. Famine ravages humans and beasts. People have to emigrate, often to places that are inhospitable to strangers. They might be outcasts. They might get enslaved. They might wind up as religious martyrs. They might be fought off.

Wells, appropriately, provide the scene for charming encounters. When there has been enough water so that crops and beasts thrive, we find fabulous celebrations. The celebrations following the barley harvest and the sheep shearing, for example, are carefree—a release from the anxieties of other seasons.

Still, much depends upon the mercy of others. Some are rich; some poor. The rich are required to give to the poor, but only on certain occasions. God, also, is counted on for mercy. People make burnt offerings and pray to win divine mercy. Yet sometimes that mercy is delayed or even withheld—as we learn in the excruciating story of Job. The God we meet in these stories can be severe—and perhaps this is one reason why these stories have been part of tradition for so long; they are as gritty and glorious as the real world.

A NOTE ON THE ILLUSTRATIONS

The illustrations in this book rely heavily on the ancient scriptures, gleaning information from various parts of the scriptures to bear on each story here. They are also informed by findings of archaeologists and biologists, including more recent work in biogenetics. For example, the people in our illustrations range in skin tone and facial characteristics. They are sometimes starkly different from Western depictions common from medieval through modern times, which were often modeled on the illustrators themselves. Skin tone is an unreliable clue to biogeography and human genetic relationships—instead, variation is common. We have therefore chosen to represent the people in these stories with the widely varying characteristics of those currently living in the areas these stories took place in—from present-day Ethiopia in Africa across the Near East.

Story 1

CREATION

GENESIS 1:1–2:4

CREATION

Darkness pressed from everywhere. Vast. Heavy. Empty.

God was alone, curled tight.

But oh, emptiness was full of potential. Like flower petals, though there were no flowers yet. But there could be. That was the point.

A wind started. It came from inside God and blew out over the waters. It cleared the way, so that God's words became inevitable: "Let there be light."

And there was light. The wondrous beginning. A crystalline start of clarity.

That was good. Night was dark. Day was light. It felt orderly, balanced. Right.

That was Night One, Day One.

But now both dark and light pressed from everywhere. And those endless waters—they lapped constantly until they couldn't be ignored any longer. Something was needed, a place to be separate from the waters. So God spoke. The words created in that marvelous way that only words can do: The heavens formed.

This was good. Order of dark and light was now accompanied by order of water and space.

That was Night Two, Day Two.

Order is a force in itself, though. One order wants another, and then another. Waters and the heavens—together they wanted more. God spoke, and the waters pulled together, leaving behind dry land. Bare like that, it revealed itself as a find, a true treasure. Land offered innumerable possibilities. God spoke, and the land filled with grasses, plants that scattered seeds that grew into more plants, and trees that bore fruit that grew into more trees. That was good. What a richness the earth allowed, what a fecundity.

That was Night Three, Day Three.

Previous: Out of interminable darkness came everything: seas and skies, mountains and valleys and jungles, and life dancing through it all.

Wind blew, a wondrous stirring, and God created light, then the heavens to waft above the waters, then dry land to nourish plants.

God looked around. That just-created earth was now lush and fragrant. Leaves fluttered in breezes from the utterly clean heavens. Colors dazzled in new-born light. All was delicious to every sense.

But now those clean, bright heavens suddenly seemed paltry in comparison—empty. Wasn't that just the way? Richness exposes poverty. Well, God could fix that. With words. God spoke, and the sun appeared, the moon, the stars. This was incredibly good. The sun had dominion over day. The moon had dominion over night. Since the moon was weaker and frailer than the sun, the stars could help shore it up with their sparkles. Together all of them could mark the passing of time—days, weeks, months, seasons, years. The patterns of time would be apparent to all. Another order. How pleasing!

That was Night Four, Day Four.

But, of course, more had to happen now. The earth and the heavens were delightful—but the waters lay still and empty. The air above that water and that earth, the air that reached to the heavens, hung flat and plain, when it should have been active, alive. Words were needed, words again; God spoke. And fish, turtles, eels, rays swam shallow and deep. Crabs scuttled. Jellyfish wavered in their flimsy-floaty way. Over those teeming waters flew pelicans, cormorants, tiny storm petrels. Over the vivid earth flew golden finches, red-headed buntings, rosy starlings. Creatures everywhere happily fed on the abundant seeds from the abundant plants. God blessed them in a way that cannot help but evoke awe: God said, "Be fruitful and multiply." Simple words. But crucial for life on earth. They bestowed on these creatures the power to make more of their own kind. To fill the seas and the air.

This was the essence of goodness.

On Day Five God filled the waters and the skies with life. All kinds of sea creatures wiggled and swam. All kinds of birds dived and soared.

That was Night Five, Day Five.

But the order of things needed more. The earth could sustain more than plant life and fowl. The earth could sustain spider, fly, snail, lizard, horse, elephant. Yes! God created all of them and it was good, right, just. Every creepy, crawly creature, docile or monstrous—all of them together! Life went flying, swooping, diving, loping, running in joyful chaos.

Ouch! Chaos! All this activity needed a ruler to impose decorum. God spoke. And humans were created in the image God trusted, God's own image. Women and men. God blessed them like the other animals: "Be fruitful and multiply." God gave them a charge: to take care of the earth, to be the masters of all, to make what God had created work.

God looked at the toils so far, including those final ones, of Night Six, Day Six. The plants were self-reproducing, ever fruitful. The animals could eat them and thrive in the pleasure of each other's company. Everything could go on forever, days melting into months, seasons, years, measured out by the sun and moon. Everything with its order. A self-sustaining creation, perpetual, perfect.

God made a judgment: finished. So on Night Seven, Day Seven, God ceased. Well done. A blessed day, this seventh one.

God rested in trust of where all this good work would lead.

THE MEASURE OF TIME

This story is based on Genesis 1, about the creation and the organization of time as it relates to nature. For example, the Earth's rotation around its axis determines the length of a day. The moon's revolution around the Earth determines the length of a month. The Earth's revolution around the sun determines the length of a year. But one part of time is not determined by nature: the breakdown of a month into weeks. The Maori of New Zealand have three 10-day intervals; northern Ethiopians, four 8-day intervals; the Wachagga of Tanzania, six 5-day intervals. Mesopotamians noted intervals of 7 days, 5 days, and 2 days, but it was the Jews who made the consistent 7-day week. Christians and Muslims adopted and spread it.

Story 2

EDEN

GENESIS 2:4–2:25

17

EDEN

God had created the world in an organized fashion. Everything had balance. But it didn't quite make sense; the picture wasn't quite complete. How could plants grow all over the earth? Plants needed rain, but God hadn't made rain. God hadn't even made springs to feed the plants from below. And God hadn't assigned anyone the task of tending those plants.

The idea that everything could thrive forever without strife or need of God's intervention was some kind of ideal based on a sense of a perfect order and a perfect justice; God knew all about order and justice.

But another side of God knew that perfection was hard to achieve. Maybe even impossible. This side of the divine—called the Lord—knew about feelings and understood mercy. The Lord didn't create solely through divine words that were clean and cold. The Lord's power to create lay in the hands—and the hands needed to get down and dirty with the materials in order to create what was needed.

This is what the Lord did.

Stomp, stomp, stomp, in the dry earth. Dust rose and the Lord fashioned a human and blew into those waiting nostrils and bestowed life. That's the way the Lord did it. Hands on.

The Lord planted a garden in the east and called it Eden. Plop! The human would live right there, smack in the middle of that garden.

The Lord made trees grow, beautiful and fruitful. Two trees were special: the Tree of Life and the Tree of Knowledge. That second tree, ah, that was the key to everything—that was the source of understanding, of knowing what is good from what is not.

For there had to be both. It was impossible to appreciate good without recognizing the lack of it. Perfection wasn't just impossible, it wasn't even desirable. It was a bore; it led to nothing—no conflict, no joy, no stories. That tree had to be there, it had to be nourished.

Previous: All of Eden, down to the tiniest detail, was fashioned from the Lord's hands: hairy fur on buffalo, striped fur on tigers, greasy fur on wolves.

Many trees grew in Eden, the most special being the Tree of Knowledge. Luscious fruits hung there, swollen and yummy— forbidden fruits.

The Lord split the land with dazzling rivers, carrying fresh water to all the plants, all the creatures. Every living thing had all it needed.

A river was needed. Well, the Lord simply made one, and split it into four streams.

One was Pishon, which wound through the land of Havilah, adorned with gold and lapis lazuli.

One was Gihon, which curved through the land of Cush.

One was Tigris, which stretched to the east of Ashur.

And the fourth was Euphrates.

And the Lord told that human—that single, blinking person—the rules, because humans, like everything else, were flawed and needed rules: "Eat from any tree in Eden. Let the juices roll down your chin in excess. Enjoy every luscious drop. But never eat from the Tree of Knowledge. For if you do, you'll be doomed to die."

The sole human kept blinking.

And the Lord realized that a human alone could accomplish little. That human needed support. So the Lord dug into the soil again and again and fashioned all beasts and all fowl, showing each one to the human and asking what would be a good name for it. Whatever name the human gave was what the creature would be called forevermore.

Yet no number of beasts or fowl was enough; the human kept blinking in that vague way. Oh, something more was needed. So the Lord cast a slumber over the human, a heavy blanket of a slumber, like a death that wasn't a death, a temporary time-out. And while the man slept, the Lord pulled a rib from the man's chest and fashioned a second human. When the man woke, he blinked no more, but stared upon this companion. "Bone of my bones," he said, entranced. "Flesh of my flesh." And he called the new human woman.

Man and woman. Formed from one flesh, separate but parts of a whole. Bare to the elements. Bare to one another. They smiled upon each other in blissful innocence.

After all, what was there to be ashamed of? Looking upon the other was like looking upon oneself.

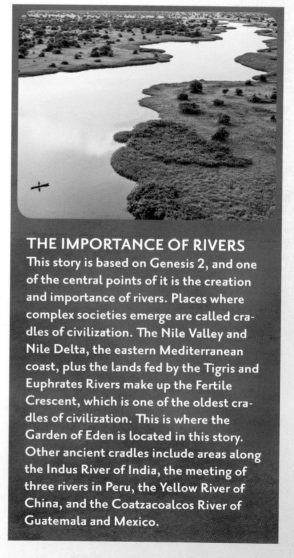

THE IMPORTANCE OF RIVERS
This story is based on Genesis 2, and one of the central points of it is the creation and importance of rivers. Places where complex societies emerge are called cradles of civilization. The Nile Valley and Nile Delta, the eastern Mediterranean coast, plus the lands fed by the Tigris and Euphrates Rivers make up the Fertile Crescent, which is one of the oldest cradles of civilization. This is where the Garden of Eden is located in this story. Other ancient cradles include areas along the Indus River of India, the meeting of three rivers in Peru, the Yellow River of China, and the Coatzacoalcos River of Guatemala and Mexico.

Story 3

EXPULSION FROM EDEN

GENESIS 3

EXPULSION FROM EDEN

A serpent inhabited the Garden of Eden, shrewd and full of unknown motives. That serpent wove his way through the fragrant plants and flicked his tongue against the woman's cheek. "Though the Lord forbade you to eat the fruit from the trees …"

"The Lord didn't say that," said the woman quickly, for though she hadn't yet been alive when the Lord told the first human the rules, she knew them. "We can eat fruit. Just not from the tree in the middle of the garden. If we eat from that tree, if we even so much as touch it, we die."

"Wrong." The serpent circled the woman and flicked his tongue against her other cheek. "You won't die. Your eyes will open. You'll know what is good from what is not, like gods do."

The tree wasn't a threat? The woman didn't take the serpent's word for it. She gazed on the tree carefully. She arrived at her own conclusion: It was a fine tree! It entranced the eyes. Certainly its fruit was good. She ate one.

She turned to her man and gave him a fruit. He ate it.

It was true: Their eyes saw differently now. What was this? They had been made from the same flesh, that was undeniable, nevertheless their flesh was different. They weren't one—they were man and woman. Naked! Like animals. But humans were meant to be special; to rise above the animals. Shame heated their cheeks. They sewed fig leaves together and clothed themselves.

They heard the Lord walking in the garden. They hid. The Lord called, "Where?" The word swirled, like the beginnings of a storm. "Where are you?"

The man answered that he was hiding from fear, for he was naked. He said this despite the fact that fig leaves now covered him.

The Lord ignored this detail, for the man's words were alarming in

Previous: The Lord had made but one rule—and the first woman broke that rule. She blamed it on the serpent that touched her cheeks. But it had been her own judgment to reach for knowledge and bear the consequences.

far more important ways. "Who told you that you were naked? Did you eat from the tree?"

"The woman that you gave to me handed me a fruit. I ate." An honest answer, though cowardly.

The Lord looked hard at the woman. "What have you done?"

"It's the serpent's fault," said the woman, matching the man in cowardice. In fact, she had judged the tree's fruit to be good on her own. But she reasoned away that fine point, for, after all, she'd have never considered that fruit if the serpent hadn't spoken to her.

"Cursed be you," said the Lord to the serpent. "From this day forth, you will be an enemy of humans. You will slither on your belly, the lowest of the low."

"And you," said the Lord to the woman, "you will know the pains and risks of having children. You will yearn for your man, and he will rule over you."

"And you," said the Lord, finally turning to the man, "did you think you'd get off free? All acts have consequences. You will eat no more from the fruits around you, picking at will. Instead, getting enough food will become the bane of your existence. You will toil in the fields. You'll fight thorn and thistle. You'll sweat for every bite of bread. All your life. Till you die. You started as dust; you'll end as dust. Dust to dust."

The man answered nothing. The consequences of being cast out of Eden were too large to comprehend in words. He needed time to live them.

But he did do one thing. Knowing now that the woman was fully distinct from him, a truly separate

Next: Eden had been dreamily easy. Leaving it behind, having to fend off who knew what—that was harsh and scary.

SERPENTS WITH LEGS
The serpent here is cursed to slither on his belly forevermore. This suggests that serpents, or snakes, originally didn't slither; they had legs. That's true. Paleontologists have established that serpents evolved from legged creatures. Some had hind legs during the late Cretaceous period, more than 66 million years ago, when dinosaurs abounded. Much of the evidence for these two-legged serpents comes from underwater geologic strata in the Middle East. It's a mystery how this knowledge was conveyed to ancient people so many millions of years later.

being, he realized he had to honor that knowledge by giving her a suitable name: He called her Eve—"mother of life."

The man and Eve. About to be cast out of the garden that had nourished them. Without defenses. Clueless.

The Lord had pity on their human frailty. Minimal pity—but pity. The Lord made them skin coats, so they wouldn't be exposed to cold and rain as they left the garden.

The woman's head whirled with worries. Might she die giving birth? Might her babes die? That's how it could be, now that she had challenged the Lord. What if her own children challenged her? What kind of a mess had she gotten humankind into?

The man couldn't think that way. His stomach growled. His eyes turned alert, searching for food. He had responsibilities.

The Lord set angels to guard the entrance to the garden behind them. Those humans must not come back. They had already eaten of the Tree of Knowledge; they already knew what was good from what was not. What if they ate of the Tree of Life and became immortal? Never! The Lord set angels and a flaming, swirling sword to guard the entrance.

There was no turning back. Carefree days were already a memory.

Story 4

THE FIRST SIBLINGS

GENESIS 4–5:5

THE FIRST SIBLINGS

The man seemed to catch on to the way life progressed among the beasts of the earth and the fowl of the air and the fish of the seas; he knew Eve as his wife, as the mother of his children to be.

Eve felt life within her—a child was there! But, being one who used her own eyes in her own way and came to her own conclusions, she decided the Lord had put that child within her. After all, the Lord was the great creator.

Eve called this newly gotten son, this strapping and lusty fellow, Cain. And she had a second son, a misty sort of son, hardly more than vapor, yet so pleasing in his vulnerability—and she called him Abel.

The children grew and shouldered responsibilities as they must. Abel herded sheep, calling to them with his wispy voice, being their gentle leader. Cain tilled the soil, flexing the muscles of his back, neck, arms, and legs, using every bit of strength he had.

Then came a time of offering to the Lord. Cain came laden with plump, aromatic fruits. Abel came laden with equally plump, though stinky, suckling lambs. And what happened? The Lord looked upon Abel and his offering, but didn't even glance at Cain or his offering. What was going on? Each son of Eve had brought the product of his labors, as was fitting. The Lord's reaction was unjust!

Anger inflamed Cain. The unappreciated. The unvalued. His face fell.

The Lord spoke in mysterious verse:

Now now, why are you mad
with a face so sad?
An offering's not a ploy
that always brings joy.

Look by the tent flap where the lion of sin
crouches, drool on his chin.
Step carefully, Cain, so you're the one to win.

Who knows what Cain thought of those words, but he turned to his brother: "Let's go out to the field." And they did. No preamble—no warning argument—just a jump: Cain was upon Abel and he slew him. Quick. Like snapping twigs. The lion had won; Cain had lost.

The Lord saw Cain and called out, "Where is your brother?" There was that word again—*where*—that word that the Lord had called out in the Garden of Eden after the serpent had done his damage. That word that pointed like the most accusing of fingers, as though the very location of the man proved his guilt.

DOMESTICATION

Cain tills the soil while Abel herds the sheep. The two activities of domesticating wild plants and wild animals are crucial to many types of human communities and helpful to other types. Relying solely on foraging and hunting for food makes a community completely vulnerable to forces it cannot control. Instead, with reasonable luck regarding climate and disease and with good practices regarding caring for land and livestock, farming and herding can provide insurance against lean seasons.

Previous: Eve's strong son, Cain, worked the fields. Her slight son, Abel, tended the sheep. Both worked hard; both did their best.

Somehow the Lord favored Abel's gifts over Cain's. The injustice wounded Cain in the very center of his being. He gave in to the evil of envy; he killed his own little brother.

The Lord punished Cain for his ill deed: He would wander for the rest of his days. His descendants thrived—but elsewhere. It was Eve's third son, Seth, whose descendants would live the stories yet to come.

But Cain said, "I don't know." His bold-faced lie soiled the air. "Am I my brother's keeper?" Now that was something different. That question hung in the stifling air. That was a question for all time. What do we owe one another? Are we each other's keepers?

"What have you done?" said the Lord. "Listen! Hear that? That's your brother's blood calling to me. You cursed the earth by spilling your brother's blood into its jaws. From this day forth, the earth will give you nothing. You can never till it again. Instead, you will wander."

"No one can survive such a punishment. Anyone I pass will kill me."

And with Cain's words, the Lord saw again the pathetic nature of these humans. Mercy stirred within the Lord's heart, as it had stirred for the first woman and the first man upon their expulsion from Eden. That's when the Lord clothed man and woman in skin coats. Now mercy made the Lord say, "Whoever kills Cain will suffer seven-fold vengeance." And the Lord put a mark upon Cain—a magic shield against harm.

So Cain wandered in the land of Nod to the east of Eden and found a wife. Where, you might ask, where, where did this wife come from? Ask away. Some answers may never be found.

Cain and his wife had a son, who in time found his own wife. That couple had a son who found a wife. And on and on. Through the years the descendants of Cain grew numerous. Some wandered. Some built cities. Some lived in tents and tended livestock. Some played the lyre and pipe. Some did metalwork.

In the meantime, the first man, now called Adam—meaning "human"—had another child with Eve, a son called Seth. And Eve believed that the Lord had given her this son to replace her slain son, Abel, the wispy, whispery one who had disappeared like vapor. Seth took a wife and had children, and all of them were in the image of the Lord. Generation after generation, it was Seth's line that would populate the world with the image of God. So it was Seth's line that mattered for posterity. Farewell to Abel, but farewell to Cain, too.

THE FLOOD

Ten generations of Seth's line rolled out through the years. They were good-looking and strong, yes, but a disappointment in terms of their hearts. Evil controlled them.

These humans brought nothing but regret to the divine. They needed to be wiped out.

But the Lord side of the divine, the side that understood feelings and was moved to mercy, took one last look at the humans. Who was that? Over there? A man full of love for family and the divine. His name was Noah. The Lord was smitten with Noah. How could all humans perish—even Noah?

Still, justice and order must prevail, for those were of utmost importance to the other side of the divine. So God decided to protect Noah and his family, but destroy all others. God told Noah to build an ark of cypress and seal it watertight with pitch. Three decks, an entrance on one side, a window at the top with a sky view. Noah, his wife, and three sons—Shem and Ham and Japheth—and their wives, plus two each of every kind of land animal and fowl, a female and a male, were all to go into the ark, along with plentiful food. Then rain would fall. And fall. Water would cover everything, just as it had in the beginning. All outside the ark would perish. The chosen few on the ark could start anew, a fresh line, a perfect future, as God had envisioned originally. This flood would undo the mistakes of creation.

A neat plan—everything fit.

But the Lord, the side of the divine emotionally attached to humans, recognized something God could not see: Evil would always lurk in the shadows. God could break what had been created, but what would come next would be equally flawed. So the Lord told Noah to take two of each creature, but he was to take seven pairs of the special creatures that were ritually pure and could be used as offerings to the divine.

Previous: Seth's descendants were wicked—all but one: Noah. So God had Noah build an ark for his wife and sons and their wives and a pair of every creature plus seven pairs of the creatures clean enough for sacrifice. An ark to ride out the coming storm.

Noah and his family built the ark, then, for a week, they worked stocking it with food, gathering the animals. Rains came. Lowlands flooded. Hills sank away. Mountaintops disappeared. For 40 nights and 40 days, it poured. When the sun showed its face again, life outside the seas had been eradicated, except the life inside that one, lonely ark. Imagine it—the confusion of beasts and fowl—the ebb and flow of hope among those few tiny humans. This storm challenged them to the core. Though the day sky was clear now and the night sky once again sparkled with stars and glowed with moon, the ordeal was not over. All that water had to subside—no small task.

God remembered Noah's family and those cringing animals closed in the ark. From within God came a wind—that wind that had begun creation on Day One. It blew across the tops of the waters and lowered them till earth appeared again. It was a new creation—a new finding of earth. For 150 days the ark bobbed along under a clean heaven as the waters gradually yielded. On the 17th day of the seventh month, the ark lodged on top of Mount Ararat.

Noah sent out a raven to find dry land. The raven flew and flew. So Noah sent out a dove. The dove returned, its bitty heart thumping so hard its chest shook. Well, they had spent so long in the ark already, Noah could be patient a bit longer. He waited a week and sent out that dove again. The dove returned with an olive leaf in its bill. Yes, the earth was drying! Noah waited another week, then sent that dove out again. The dove didn't return; Noah imagined the bird cooing in the dizziness of freedom. Soon, oh so soon, the ark inhabitants could disembark. Everyone inside crowded against the door, but Noah made them wait, for he was faithful, loyal, obedient; they waited nearly two months. At last, God told Noah it was time. Humans and beasts walked out onto the washed earth. Fowl flew out across the scrubbed sky.

Forty days of rain, 150
days of bobbing under
a clear sky, two months
of land slowly drying—
Noah's family and all
those animals waited
and wondered. Then
they emerged to a clean
earth under a rainbow
of promise.

It was time, again, to be fruitful and multiply.

But first Noah had a task; now he understood why the Lord had made him bring extra pairs of the ritually pure animals. Noah built an altar and sacrificed those pure beasts and fowl to the Lord. The Lord smelled that delectable aroma and vowed never again to bring such destruction. From thence forward, days and nights would follow one another as the orderly God had planned on Day One. The Lord promised that the sun and moon would always mark the passing of weeks, months, seasons, years—a reliable pattern—just as the orderly God had planned on Night Four, Day Four.

The earth would feed the people, just as God had planned.

But other food was needed, too. Flesh. Death was an omnipresent reality now. Humans had brought it upon themselves. They would kill animals and eat them. A gruesome reality. The Lord side accepted this reality because humans were weak—the Lord had always known that.

But what about the God side? God looked anew at everything and finally understood the human condition. The Lord was right. God told Noah that he and his kind could eat the flesh of clean beasts and

fowl, so long as their blood was first spilled on the earth; the life force in blood should return to the earth, from whence it had come.

God made the same covenant with humans that the Lord had made. Never again would God wreak such destruction. As a sign of this promise, God pulled back the string of the divine bow and shot into the heavens.

Colors dazzled everyone.

There would be cloudy days ahead, for humans would transgress and God would be disappointed. But the sun would shine through and God would curb divine righteous anger. That rainbow would forever be a reminder to God to keep the promise not to destroy humanity.

The two sides of the divine found a common peace.

RAINBOWS

Rainbows consist of raindrops and sunlight. As light enters a droplet, it is bent. Inside, the curved, mirrorlike sides of the droplet reflect the light. As the light emerges, it is bent again. This makes the curve of a rainbow, which would be a full circle if the surface of the earth didn't get in the way. Sunlight is made up of all colors. But different colors bend different amounts of light, so the colors split, making the rainbow a range of all colors. You will always view rainbows with sunlight behind you and rain ahead.

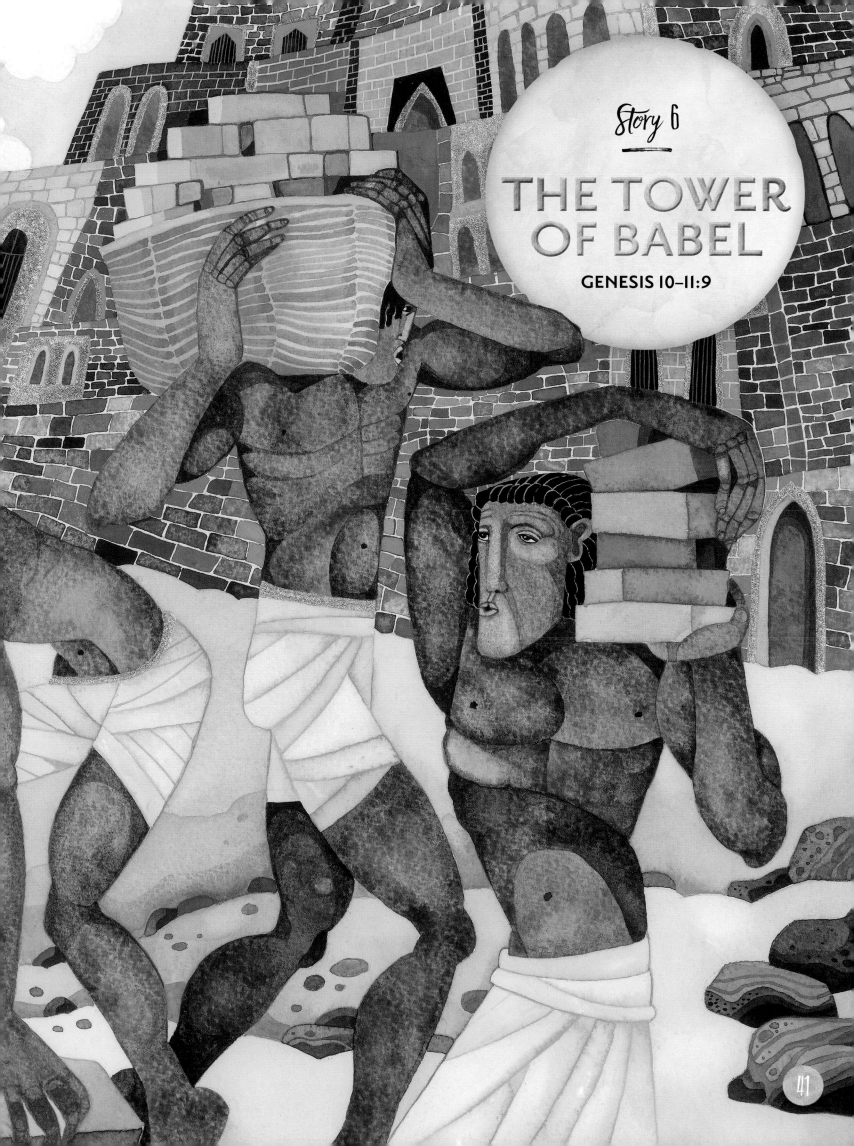

THE TOWER OF BABEL

GENESIS 10–11:9

THE TOWER OF BABEL

Noah's line begot generation after generation. Soon the mountain range was ajumble with people cooking and singing and working together as storytellers regaled them with tales of the past. And what a past it was! They shivered at the thought. After each rainfall they ran outside to scan the sky, and sighed in relief when the rainbow arched there. The Lord was keeping the covenant. They trusted in that. No more floods would come—no more purges of humanity. Still, they would do nothing to alarm the Lord. They were ever aware that cooperation was their strength. Never again would they fall into evil ways that might tempt the Lord to act against them.

After 10 generations had passed, the descendants of Noah had grown so populous that the mountains did not offer a place where all of them could gather easily. That was cause for concern; a scattered people could never be as strong as a united people. So they traveled from the east, from the old country, to a valley in the land of Shinar. Rich, black land stretched out in a flat plain between two rivers. What a fine place to settle.

"Come on!" they said to one another. "Let's bake bricks! Let's burn them hard." And so they baked bricks white and hard as stone.

"Come on!" they said again. "Let's build a city with a tower whose head is in the heavens." Ha! That would be a way to make a name for themselves, a united identity as a settled people, so they should never scatter in the future, so they should grow stronger and stronger.

HUMAN LANGUAGES
At least 100,000 years ago, *Homo sapiens*, the species that modern humans belong to, developed speech. However, they were gesturing to each other probably another 100,000 years earlier. Perhaps the gestures of early *Homo sapiens* were organized enough to be considered language. When these humans broke into communities and moved far away from one another, their language changed. (Languages always change through contact with other languages, through social differences, and through natural processes in usage.) Today there are around 7,000 spoken languages and more (perhaps many more) than 200 sign languages.

That's exactly what they set about doing.

The Lord came down and walked through the area, looking at the homes and meeting halls already built and at those in mid-construction. The Lord circled the looming tower. And the Lord realized that this ability of humankind to work together made them a formidable force. Indeed, if they set their minds to it, they could accomplish anything now.

That thought was unsettling. Humans were unpredictable. Undisciplined. Unwise. Their power needed to be checked.

How had humans come to this point?

Because the people shared a language, they could cooperate on making a tower tall enough to reach the heavens. The Lord worried: What might these humans try next?

Language! Just look at them. Look at their hands, at their faces, at their lips. They talked to one another easily. Why, they chattered, sharing their hopes and fears, making elaborate plans. Language allowed them to understand each other—to empathize. Language allowed them to organize and act as one. Language was the dangerous power.

"Come on!" said the Lord. "Let's go down and baffle them. Let's give them each a different way of expressing themselves, so they can't understand each other."

Who was the Lord calling to? Perhaps the God side of the divine? Another question that may remain unanswered.

And so the Lord changed that most fundamental of human powers: language.

The humans woke and turned to one another for conversation, just as on past days. No. It was not to be. They understood one another partially or not at all. They couldn't tell jokes, they couldn't complain, they couldn't find joy and solace in each other. They were unable to help one another.

Confounded and bewildered, they left off building that city and that tower. They scattered over the earth, though they knew in their hearts that scattering only weakened them. What choice did they have? The binding power of language was lost.

They called the city that they left behind Babylon, for it was a source of confusion—*balal*.

What had happened? Why why why?

Humans had so much wanted to fuse, to make a unity that felt desirable to them. But it wasn't to be. Humans were meant to be fruitful and multiply and inhabit this whole wonderful world. Just as Adam and Eve had to leave Eden and find their own ways, create their own stories, so the descendants of Noah had to leave Babylon and give us the stories that follow.

When the people woke and found they all had different languages, they couldn't work together anymore. Dumbfounded, they gathered their belongings and left, scattering across the lands.

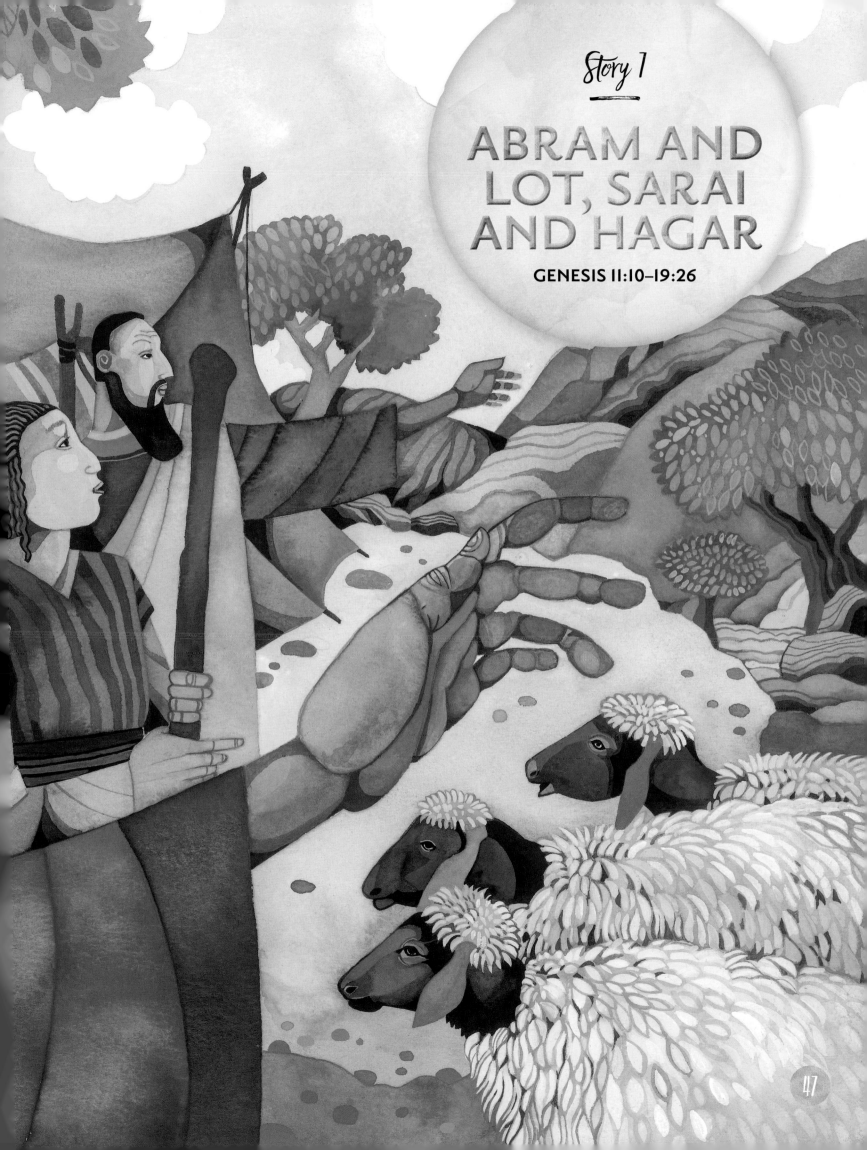

ABRAM AND LOT, SARAI AND HAGAR

GENESIS 11:10–19:26

ABRAM AND LOT, SARAI AND HAGAR

The next 10 generations of Noah made large families in order to fill the earth. In that 10th generation was Abram, who took Sarai as his wife, but she gave him no children. An ache lodged in Abram's heart. But Abram loved his beautiful Sarai and contented himself with the idea that his orphaned nephew Lot might serve as heir.

When Abram was 75, the Lord told him to leave his land, his birthplace, his father's home. The Lord would bless him and show him a new home. Abram gathered Sarai and Lot, and left, along with sheep, cattle, donkeys, camels, tents, servants. Lot had amassed wealth, which meant the entourage was impressive, indeed. When they arrived in Canaan, the Lord told Abram this was his land.

That land served Abram for years, though at one point there was famine, and all had to sojourn in Egypt. But they soon returned to Canaan, along with Hagar, an Egyptian handmaid for Sarai.

After a while, Abram's herdsmen argued with Lot's herdsmen, saying the land could not support them all. Lot stayed silent; so Abram had to find a resolution.

Abram suggested they move to different lands. "If you go left, I'll go right. If you go right, I'll go left."

Lot eyed the plain of the River Jordan. Well-watered, green, and lush. As fertile as Egypt. As Eden, even! Lot took his servants and animals and moved. He pitched his tent leaning toward the nearby city of Sodom, though he knew that city was corrupt. The fertile land was too good to pass up. Lot made a family there.

Abram stayed behind in Canaan. The Lord gave him all the land he could see to fill with family. "It will be as hard to count your offspring as to count the dust of the earth."

Previous: Abram and his wife Sarai moved to the land of Canaan, with all their animals and workers, and with Abram's nephew Lot and all his animals and workers. But the land couldn't hold them all, so Lot continued on to the fertile land in the plain of the River Jordan.

Abram listened, baffled. He and Sarai were old. What offspring?

Soon a man arrived and called Abram a Hebrew—a word that marked him as an immigrant. The man told Abram that over in the River Jordan's plain his nephew Lot had trouble. The neighboring cities of Sodom and Gomorrah were at war with other kingdoms. These city people lived lawless, robbing one another. They couldn't unite, and now the armies of four kings had raided them—taking prisoners, among them Lot. Abram and his workers quickly rallied and rescued the hapless prisoners.

Life went back to how it had been—with Lot and his wife and now several daughters living near Sodom, and Abram and Sarai living in Canaan.

The Lord came again to Abram with talk about his future family, who would have a difficult time for hundreds of years, but then would prevail. The Lord told Abram, "It will be as hard to count your offspring as to count the stars."

This talk made no sense to Abram.

Then, to top it off, Sarai came to Abram, longing for a child. She had a plan. If only Abram would have a child with Sarai's handmaid Hagar, Sarai could act as mother to the child, with the status of a mother with a son.

How could such a plan work out? Yet Abram would try.

Hagar became pregnant. Instantly, the handmaid felt superior to her mistress. Sarai couldn't bear being looked down on, so she harassed Hagar. Hagar fled. A task messenger of the Lord—an angel—found Hagar by a desert spring and told her to return, for Hagar would bear a son named Ishmael. The name meant that the divine would always hear the boy. Hagar returned, and gave birth to Ishmael.

LARGE FAMILIES
The need to multiply and inhabit the earth recurs in these ancient stories, where being barren resulted in personal sadness and more: true hardship. God's first blessing to the first man and woman was "Be fruitful and multiply." The generations to come were to take care of the earth, in reverence and respect for all that had been created. These were times of high death rates, due to injuries and disease. Large families were the foundation for having the workforce to do the essential farming for the community and to stand firm against enemies.

When Abram was 99, God renamed him Abraham. The addition of that letter *h* added the breath of God. Sarai was renamed Sarah, so God's breath was within her, too. Then God commanded that Abraham circumcise himself and all his herdsmen as a sign of their covenant to trust God forever.

God told Abraham that he and Sarah would have a son of their own. Abraham fell down laughing. He was nearly 100. Sarah was 90. He said to God, "If only Ishmael could be the one you favor."

God assured Abraham that Ishmael would have a wonderful future. But Abraham's son with Sarah was the one that God's covenant was with. That son would be called Isaac—laughter. Abraham thought of how he'd laughed at God's promise. Still, loyal Abraham did as God asked.

Soon three men appeared to Abraham as he sat in the shade near his tent entrance on a hot day. Abraham knew these men were the Lord. He brought them water to bathe their feet. He called to Sarah to make bread. He chose a fat calf to roast. He feted the men on bread, roast, milk, and curds. They promised he'd have a son with Sarah. Old Sarah listened from the tent and laughed in disbelief.

Then the three men, who were, in fact, the Lord, told Abraham that Sodom and Gomorrah were said to be pits of violence. The Lord prepared to send task messengers ahead to make sure this outcry was true before destroying both cities.

Abraham's chest went cold; his nephew Lot's family lived there. "Shall not the judge of all deal justly? What if there are fifty innocent people there? Would you destroy the place?"

"If there are fifty innocent, I will not destroy the place."

"What about forty-five?" When the Lord said no, Abraham asked, "What about forty?" They negotiated in this way down to 10. If the task messengers found even 10 innocent people, the cities would not be destroyed.

Sodom was a place where people lost their ability to tell what was right from what was not. The Lord set it afire. Lot and his wife and two daughters were told to flee and not look back. But Lot's wife erred; she looked back and turned to salt.

When the Lord sent two task messengers to Sodom, they came across Lot sitting at the city gate. Lot graciously fed these visitors, just as Abraham had done when the Lord visited him. Soon Sodomites surrounded the house—all thugs who demanded these visitors come out. Lot trembled. In panic, he offered his two unmarried daughters to the crowd if they'd leave the visitors in peace. An abomination of an offer. Perhaps Lot had lived too long near those violent people.

The task messengers shot out a brilliant flash that blinded the thugs, so they could not find their way into Lot's home. They told Lot to leave immediately. Lot ran to his married daughters in town and begged them to flee. His sons-in-law thought this was a joke; they refused.

The task messengers urged Lot to flee and not look back. Lot and his wife and two unmarried daughters fled.

The area behind them filled with brimstone, fire, and smoke, as terrifying as the flood Noah's family had endured. The noise was deafening; the heat, stifling. Lot's wife, ah, the poor woman made the mistake of looking back. She'd been raised in Sodom— she had no practice obeying the Lord. One glance, and she transformed into a pillar of salt, a monument of dried tears.

Story 8

ABRAHAM, ISHMAEL, ISAAC

GENESIS 21–22

ABRAHAM, ISHMAEL, ISAAC

Sarah, agog at her own aged body, gave birth to Isaac. When the child was weaned, Abraham threw a feast.

At the feast, Sarah saw Ishmael laughing. Ishmael could have been laughing for many reasons. But Sarah still smarted at how Hagar had acted haughty toward her years before; she was primed to take offense at Hagar's son Ishmael. She told Abraham to cast out Ishmael—just as Adam and Eve were cast out of Eden.

Ishmael was Abraham's firstborn. How could he do this?

But God told Abraham to obey Sarah, for Ishmael, too, would have a grand future.

Abraham rose early to shoulder the burden of casting out Ishmael. He found bread. He filled a skin bag with water. He gave these to Hagar. He clumped slowly, like a man in the most horrible of dreams. He told the woman to leave with her son—his son.

Hagar and Ishmael wandered outside town into the wilderness of Beersheba. The sun scorched the earth. They drank the water, but it barely helped. Soon it was gone. They were doomed. Hagar left Ishmael under a bush and sat a bowshot distance away, so she would not see her son die. And though she was dry as a bone, she wept.

Ishmael, too, cried out.

That was the saving grace. His name assured that the divine would always hear him. God's task messengers told Hagar not to fear. God opened Hagar's eyes. There before her was a well. Hagar filled the skin bag and Ishmael drank. God watched over him as he grew into a man, a fine bowman, who lived in the wilderness with his mother and, eventually, with his wife, who, like his mother, was Egyptian.

But casting out Ishmael—being loyal to God even in such a harsh deed—wasn't the end of Abraham's suffering. God now called, "Abraham."

Previous: Hagar, the handmaid of Sarah, was lost in the wilderness with her son Ishmael, Abraham's first son. They were near death from lack of water. But when Ishmael cried out, God heard him. A well appeared, and Hagar and Ishmael drew water from the well in a skin bag and survived.

"Here I am."

"Go. Take your son …"

I have two sons, thought Abraham.

"… your only son …"

Each is the only son to his mother, thought Abraham.

"… the one you love …"

I love them both, thought Abraham.

"Isaac. Take him to a mountain peak. Sacrifice him as a burnt offering to me."

Abraham had always done everything God asked. He would shoulder this burden, too, hideous though it was. He rose early. He saddled his donkey. He fetched two servant boys. He got Isaac. He split wood for the burnt offering. Clump, clump, clump, through this slow dreadful dream. They walked three days till God said they had arrived. Abraham told the servant boys to wait with the donkey. He put the wood on Isaac's shoulder and he carried fire and the cleaver. The two of them walked as one, up the mountain.

"Father …" said Isaac.

"Here I am, my son."

"We have the fire and the wood. But where is the sheep for offering?"

Abraham's throat was raw. His heart flamed. "God will see to the offering"—he swallowed—"my son."

The two of them walked as one to the mountaintop. Abraham built an altar. Clump, clump. Each step was like a killing blow. He laid out the firewood. Clump, clump. He bound his son Isaac—clump—placed him on the altar on top of the wood—clump—curled his fingers around

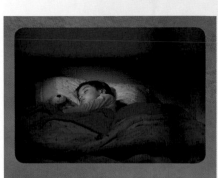

MOVEMENT IN DREAMS
In this story God demands Abraham sacrifice his son Isaac. Abraham moves slowly, clumping along, as though he's in a dream. In fact, time does feel like it is passing more slowly in dreams than in wakefulness. This might be because action in a dream lacks the muscular feedback of action when we are awake, so the brain needs more time to process it. Or it might be because the sleeping brain is simply slower and more sluggish, so action is processed slowly and sluggishly.

the grip of the cleaver. It felt heavy as a boulder, heavy enough to crush him. Yet he held it tight. He could hardly see for the tears.

"Abraham, Abraham," came an urgent, heavenly voice.

"Here I am," said Abraham. He swiped at his eyes.

"Stop. Do nothing to the boy. Now I know you are in awe of God, for you don't withhold even your son from me."

Abraham lifted his eyes and saw a ram caught by his horns in a bush. That ram became the burnt offering instead of Isaac.

"Because you have done this, you will have more offspring than stars in the heavens and grains of sand on the seashore. I will bless all of them."

Abraham returned home. The moon was still alternating with the sun—so day followed night. Plants were still growing. Rain still fell now and then. Breath still moved in and out of Abraham's lungs, of Isaac's lungs. They were alive. All went on. Abraham even learned that back at his old home, his relatives were thriving. His brother's son had grown by now and had a daughter named Rebekah. All went on.

But it would never be the same. Abraham had been ready to slay Isaac, though he loved him. Isaac's eyes still burned from the salt of his father's tears as he had leaned over the boy with that cleaver.

No, it would never be the same.

Abraham was ready to obey God's most searing order and kill Isaac—his Isaac, his dear son with Sarah. At the last moment, God relented, and a ram appeared, to be sacrificed in Isaac's stead.

STORY 9

REBEKAH

GENESIS 24

REBEKAH

Soon after the binding of Isaac, his mother, Sarah, died, perhaps of grief at what had almost happened to her son at the hand of her husband. Abraham was very old now, and he looked at his motherless son and decided Isaac needed a wife before Abraham, too, should die. So he told his servant Eliezer to return to Nahor, the homeland where he and Sarah had grown up, and fetch a wife for Isaac.

"But what if the woman won't come with me?" asked Eliezer. "Should I then send Isaac himself to fetch her?"

"No. Isaac must not go there." Abraham told Eliezer that a task messenger of the Lord would pave the way for him. And if the woman still refused to come, then Eliezer would be free of his obligation.

So the servant loaded gifts onto 10 of Abraham's camels and traveled to Nahor. He arrived in the evening and had his camels kneel near the well of the bubbling spring. The townspeople's daughters came at that hour to draw water. Eliezer prayed about an imagined encounter. He'd say to a young woman, "Please lower your jar that I may drink," and she would answer, "Drink. And I'll water your camels, too." Yes, the woman who answered that way would be the right bride for Isaac.

And here came Rebekah, beautiful, glowing daughter of Betuel, son of Milcah, the wife of Abraham's brother. She had a water jug perched on her shoulder. The sunlight sparkled off the beads of water that had formed on the outside of that jug in the hot air. It was heavy, no doubt, but the girl carried it as though effortlessly.

Eliezer imagined the cool spring water inside, sloshing as she walked and his mouth felt parched. "Please lower your jar that I may drink," said Eliezer.

"Drink." Rebekah lowered her jar and watched Eliezer slake his thirst. "I'll water your camels, too." She poured jug after jug of water into the camel trough.

Previous: Abraham's servant Eliezer went to Nahor to find the right wife for Isaac. He set a test in his head: If he asked a young woman for water and she gave water not just to him but also to his camels, this would be the just bride. He was right. Rebekah was perfect for Isaac.

Eliezer gave Rebekah a gold nose ring and two gold bracelets, and asked who she was and if there was room in her home for him to pass the night.

Rebekah said she was the child of Betuel, the son of Milcah, and assured Eliezer that they had fodder for the camels and a room for him. She ran ahead and told her mother what had happened.

Rebekah's brother Laban looked at the gold jewelry and rushed out to the well to bring the man home with him to eat and sleep. But Eliezer needed to tell them his message before he would eat. So he told them the whole story—of Sarah giving birth to Isaac in her old age and how Isaac now needed a wife from this place—the homeland of Sarah and Abraham—not from the land of the Canaanites, where Isaac now lived. Eliezer described Abraham's considerable wealth and he repeated the words that Abraham and he had exchanged, about what to do if the woman Eliezer found was not willing to come with him. He told about his prayer of finding a woman who would give water to both him and his camels. On and on he went, describing how Rebekah had been the exact answer to his prayers—and how the discovery that she was the granddaughter of Abraham's brother meant all of it had happened just as it should have.

CAMELS
This is the second time we've seen camels—Abram and Sarai brought camels when they left their homeland originally. These were probably one-humped dromedaries, used primarily for transportation of goods. By around 1200 B.C.E. saddles appeared, so camels could also be ridden. Camels have two rows of eyelashes and three eyelids, to keep sand out of their eyes. They have fur that keeps sand out of their ears. Their nostrils close between breaths to keep sand out of their throats. Thus, they are perfectly designed for desert living.

Isaac was contemplating in a field when Rebekah saw him. Somehow she knew this man would mean something to her. She got off her camel and learned that the man in the field was her future husband.

Laban and his father Betuel told Eliezer, "Here is Rebekah. She is yours."

So Eliezer bowed low and gave Rebekah and her brother and her mother silver and gold jewelry and costly and precious cloths. Then he ate and slept.

In the morning Laban and his mother hesitated. They wanted Rebekah to stay home another 10 days before journeying.

Eliezer begged them not to delay; his master was waiting.

At this point they turned to Rebekah, the one to whom all of this mattered the most, to ask what she wanted.

The lovely Rebekah said, "I will go."

Her family blessed her, wishing her many children who would inherit the gates of their enemies.

So Rebekah and her handmaids climbed on the camels and left with Eliezer.

Isaac, meanwhile, had returned from a visit to the very well where Hagar had saved Ishmael. He was meditating in a field at home—simply being alone as a man of 40 years will do—when he looked up and saw camels approaching.

Rebekah was on one of those camels. She lifted her eyes and saw Isaac, and she slid from the camel and asked Eliezer, "Who is that man?"

"My master."

So Rebekah covered herself in her shawl.

Eliezer told Isaac the whole story, yet again. He told about his prayer and about the girl who gave water generously to both him and his camels. He repeated it as though this third telling would seal the event as a truth that couldn't be questioned: Rebekah was meant for Isaac.

Isaac brought Rebekah home to his mother's tent—still full of grief from the old woman's death—and he married her and loved her. Yes, she was welcome comfort after such sorrow.

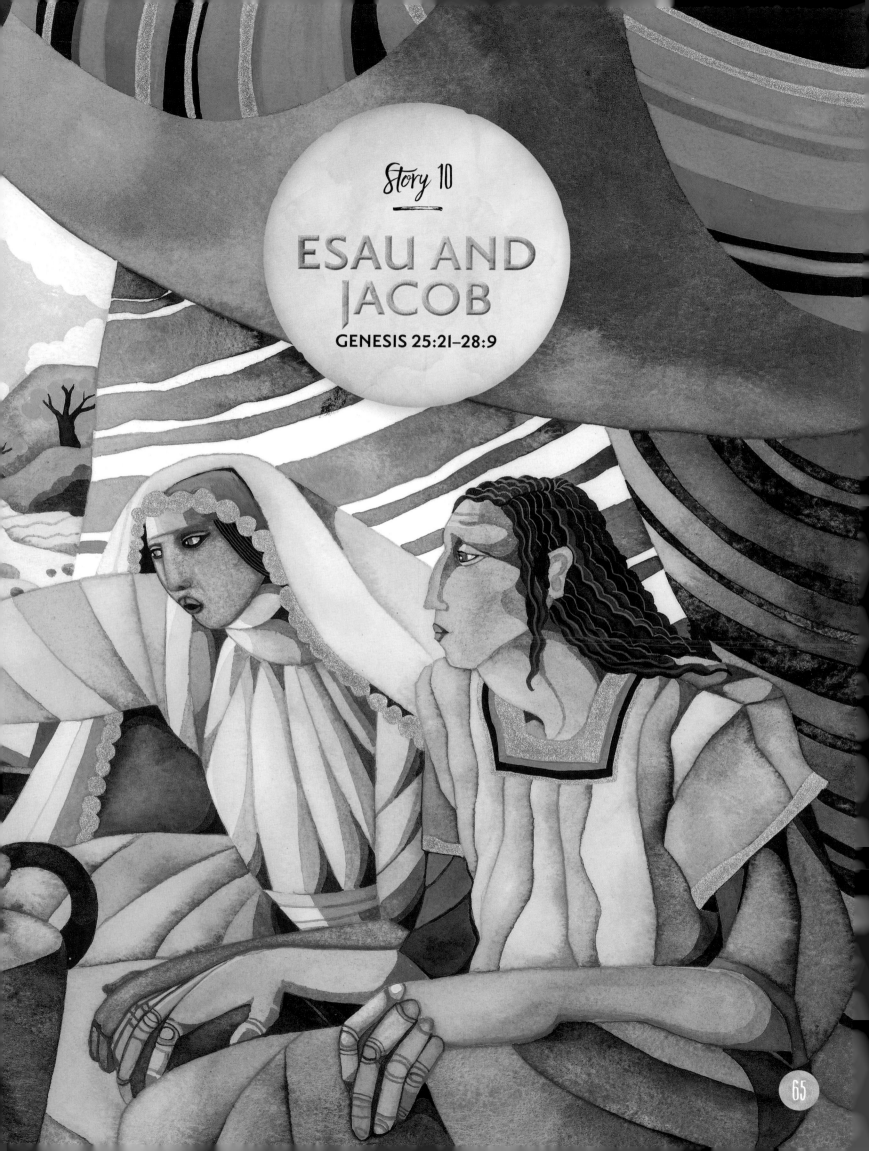

Story 10

ESAU AND JACOB

GENESIS 25:21–28:9

ESAU AND JACOB

Rebekah, like Sarah, had trouble conceiving. Isaac pleaded with the Lord, and Rebekah became pregnant with twins. They tussled inside her. In her discomfort, Rebekah went to the Lord complaining, "Why me?"

The Lord told her each twin "would lead a nation, and the elder would serve the younger."

This message was an echo. Abel had been Cain's younger brother—and the Lord had gazed upon him, not upon Cain. Isaac had been Ishmael's younger brother—and God's covenant had been with Isaac, not with Ishmael. Rebekah responded to that echo; her heart cleaved to whichever child would be born second.

The firstborn had red hair all over, like a coat. They called him Esau. The second-born came out clinging to his brother's heel. They named him Jacob, which meant "heel."

Esau became a hunter, always outside. Isaac loved him best because of the tasty game dishes he brought home. Jacob became a tent-dweller, a homebody. Rebekah loved him best—with that steadiness that Abraham had felt for Isaac.

It was as though each parent had only one son.

Meanwhile Abraham took another wife and had other children. When he died, his firstborn, Ishmael, and his second-born, Isaac, buried him beside his first wife, Sarah.

Soon after, back in Canaan, Jacob made a red lentil stew—with bubbles from the bottom of the pot turning everything tipsy-turvy, like a rebellion, releasing an aroma so fine, it dizzied the birds. Esau came home exhausted and famished. He begged Jacob for that stew.

"Sell me your birthright," said Jacob.

Esau might have laughed—the right of the firstborn in exchange for a bowl of stew? But what did the firstborn's right amount to, anyway? Esau would die, just as Abraham had. Human life was a flash of

Previous: Isaac's first son, Esau, brought home animals for his mother, Rebekah, to cook into stews. His younger brother Jacob stayed at home instead.

light—here and gone. So Esau agreed. He ate Jacob's stew and gave up his birthright.

Many years later, when elderly Isaac's eyes were bleary, he called out, "My son."

"Here I am," said Esau, knowing he was the son Isaac had always needed.

Isaac told Esau to hunt game and make him a savory dish before he died. Then he would bless Esau.

Esau left for the fields.

Rebekah had overheard. She wanted that blessing for Jacob. She told Jacob about the promised blessing and ordered him to bring her two choice goat kids for a stew. Then Jacob could pretend to be Esau, bring the stew to Isaac, and receive the blessing.

"Esau is hairy," said Jacob. "I am smooth. Father will know I'm a trickster. He'll curse me."

"If there's a curse, it falls on me," said Rebekah.

Jacob fetched the goat kids. Rebekah made the stew. She dressed Jacob in Esau's clothes. She put the hairy goat pelts on Jacob's hand and neck.

Disguised, Jacob went to Isaac's bedside. "Father."

LENTILS

In this story, Esau gives up his birthright for a lentil stew. Lentils were an essential food in biblical times and are still widely eaten today. One of the first cultivated crops, they were grown from present-day Bangladesh, westward across India, Pakistan, the Arabian Peninsula, Egypt, and around the coast of the Mediterranean Sea. Lentils grow without special attention, and rotate well with grains to keep a field fertile. They are high in protein and the dried plants make good animal fodder. Lentils are even used in traditional medicine.

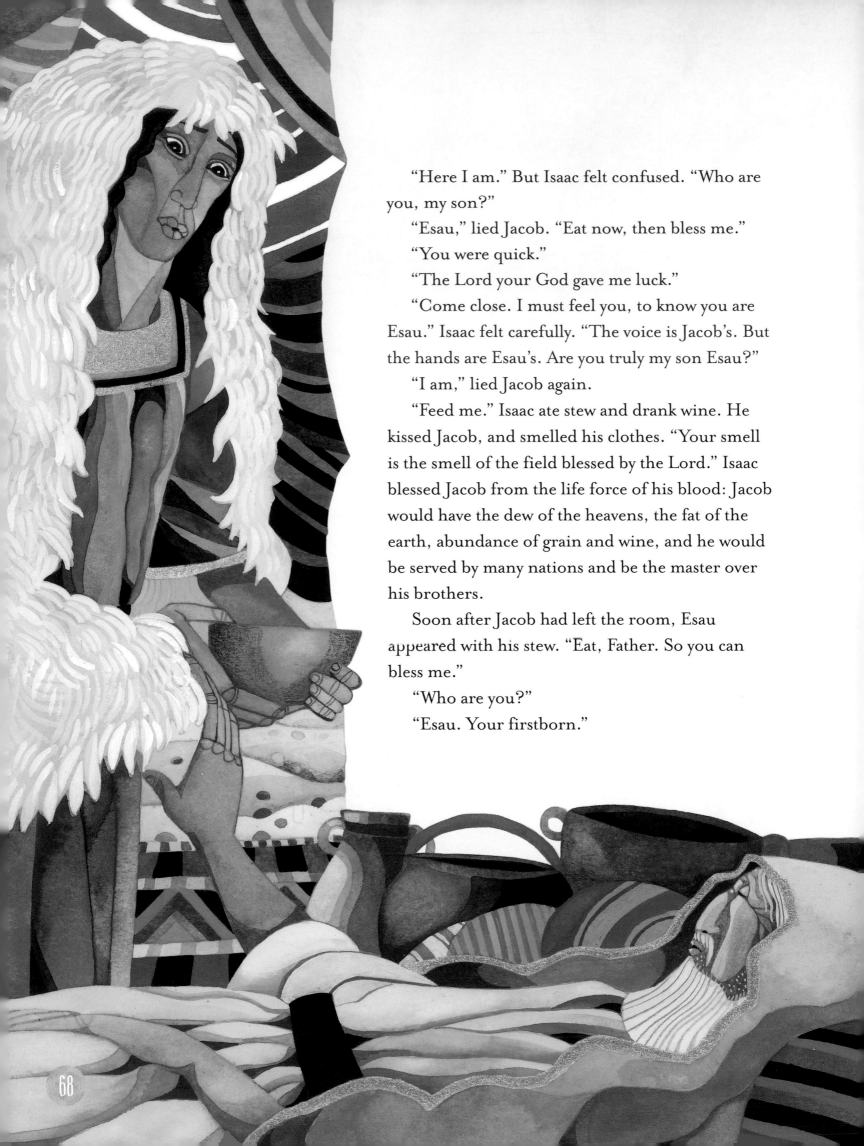

"Here I am." But Isaac felt confused. "Who are you, my son?"

"Esau," lied Jacob. "Eat now, then bless me."

"You were quick."

"The Lord your God gave me luck."

"Come close. I must feel you, to know you are Esau." Isaac felt carefully. "The voice is Jacob's. But the hands are Esau's. Are you truly my son Esau?"

"I am," lied Jacob again.

"Feed me." Isaac ate stew and drank wine. He kissed Jacob, and smelled his clothes. "Your smell is the smell of the field blessed by the Lord." Isaac blessed Jacob from the life force of his blood: Jacob would have the dew of the heavens, the fat of the earth, abundance of grain and wine, and he would be served by many nations and be the master over his brothers.

Soon after Jacob had left the room, Esau appeared with his stew. "Eat, Father. So you can bless me."

"Who are you?"

"Esau. Your firstborn."

"But who then already fed me?" Isaac trembled. "I gave him my blessing. It stays." Blessings cannot be undone.

Esau twisted in pain. He was Isaac's favorite. He was the one Isaac turned to for good food. They loved one another deeply. This could not be. "Bless me, too, Father."

"Your brother stole your blessing."

"Jacob took my birthright and now he's taken my blessing! Oh, Father, have you no blessing left for me?"

"I made him master over you. I blessed him with grain and wine. What do I have left to bless you with?"

Something. Anything. Just one blessing from this father who was so dear to him. Esau wept. "Bless me, too."

Isaac rallied. He blessed Esau with the dew of the heavens and the fat of the earth. But he said Esau would live by his sword and serve his brother. Yet one day Esau would rebel, and break free of the yoke that his brother had placed on his neck.

Poor Esau muttered that once Isaac died, he would kill his brother Jacob.

Rebekah, ever the eavesdropper like Sarah before her, told Jacob to flee fast. He must go live with her brother in her homeland until Esau's wrath should subside. But first, she convinced Isaac to warn Jacob not to marry a Hittite woman here in Canaan. Esau had taken two Hittite wives and Rebekah couldn't bear them. She'd be bereft if Jacob did the same. So Isaac told Jacob to marry a woman from Rebekah's homeland. This time he blessed Jacob truly, knowing who he was.

By chance, Esau heard this exchange. He hadn't realized his mother didn't like his wives. So he went to Ishmael, Isaac's half-brother, and married one of his daughters. Poor Esau, he was unaware of the friction between Ishmael and Isaac. Esau could never do anything right.

Jacob covered himself in a goat pelt and served his father, Isaac, a stew, pretending to be Esau. Fooled by the feel and smell of him, Isaac gave Jacob the blessing he had intended to give Esau.

JACOB, RACHEL, LEAH

**GENESIS 28:10–33,
35:16–35:20**

JACOB, RACHEL, LEAH

Jacob left his parents, Isaac and Rebekah, in Canaan, and traveled toward Rebekah's homeland, the homeland of his grandfather Abraham. Along the way he stopped in a spot that felt so holy, he thought of it as "the place." He stayed the night, using a stone for his pillow.

And he dreamed, oh, did he dream. The dream came slow and heavy and real, as though saying, "Here I am." A ladder appeared with its foot stretching earthward and its top stretching heavenward—like the top of the tower of Babel. Task messengers went up and down that ladder. "I am the Lord," came the heavenly voice, "the God of Abraham and Isaac." This voice blessed Jacob: His offspring would spread out like the dust of the earth.

Jacob was awestruck. The ladder was the gateway to heaven. Isaac's blessing had not been an accident; the Lord was with Jacob. In the morning, Jacob poured oil over his pillow stone and named the place Bethel. If the Lord brought him safely home, Bethel would become the house of God and Jacob would tithe to God forever.

Bursting with gratitude, Jacob arrived in his mother's homeland in search of her brother Laban. He came upon a well with three flocks of sheep around it. A huge stone covered the well mouth. All the shepherds had to work together to move that stone aside for the sheep to drink. Jacob asked the shepherds if they knew Laban.

They did. Furthermore, Laban's young daughter Rachel was now driving her sheep to the well.

Jacob saw that amazing girl and energy shot through him. He moved the huge stone from the well. Then he swept Rachel into his arms and kissed her. And wept, while the astonished girl watched. He explained he was the son of her aunt Rebekah.

Rachel ran to tell her father, Laban, who ran to welcome Jacob: "You are my bone and my flesh."

Previous: Jacob ran away to the land of his mother. There he stopped at a well and moved aside a huge stone that normally took three men to move. Where did his energy come from? He was already smitten with the girl watching him—his cousin Rachel.

Jacob fell to working for Laban. After a month, Laban asked what recompense he wanted. Laban had two daughters, beautiful Rachel and her older sister, Leah, with the soft eyes. Jacob was in a long line of people who knew love. Abraham had loved his wife Sarah and his son Isaac. Isaac loved his wife Rebekah. Rebekah loved her son Jacob. Jacob already loved Rachel. He asked to marry her. Laban agreed, if Jacob worked for him for seven years.

Seven years passed as though days, because Jacob's love was so strong. Then they wed. That night, Laban brought his daughter into Jacob's tent. But in the morning, Jacob saw the truth: The woman beside him was Leah, not Rachel. Jacob, who had tricked Isaac into giving him Esau's blessing, had now been tricked himself. He cried out, "Why?" Laban said that younger daughters were never married off before older ones. If Jacob waited a week, he could take Rachel as his second wife, but he must work seven more years. Jacob agreed, and so within a week both daughters were his wives.

Then the babies came. Leah gave birth to Reuben—which meant "see, a son." She hoped Jacob would love her for this heir. She gave birth to Simeon—which meant "God has heard." How could Jacob not love her now? She gave birth to Levi—which meant "will join." Three sons were a grand gift. Jacob had to love her. But Jacob's heart was cold marble. Leah's soft, tender eyes hurt constantly. She had a fourth son, Judah—which meant "sing praise"—for she realized it was only God she could count on for love. She stopped having children.

Jacob married Leah, but he never loved her. She gave him son after son, but nothing she could do would soften his heart toward her.

Meanwhile, the beauty Rachel was barren. She demanded of Jacob, "Give me sons. If you don't, I am dead."

"What? Am I God?" For this barrenness was not Jacob's doing.

Rachel found a solution. She could offer her handmaid Bilhah to Jacob as a third wife, like her husband's grandmother Sarah had offered her handmaid to Abraham. If Bilhah had a son, Rachel could have the status of mother to that child.

Bilhah soon bore a son. Rachel named him Dan, which meant "God judged in my favor." Bilhah bore another son. Rachel named him Naphtali, which meant "I fought and won." Alas, Rachel was in a battle of babies with her sister Leah.

Leah offered her own handmaid, Zilpah, to Jacob as a fourth wife.

If Jacob was aware of the growing strain in his household, he didn't show it. Soon Zilpah had a son, who Leah named Gad, which meant "good luck has come." Zilpah had another son. Leah named him Asher, which meant "good fortune." Now Jacob had eight sons, none by the envious, yet still beautiful, Rachel.

One day Reuben, Leah's oldest son, came home from the field with an armload of mandrakes, a plant known for making people fertile. Rachel wanted them terribly. She bartered with Leah for them—Rachel would get the mandrakes, Leah would get more time with Jacob.

Leah told Jacob she'd hired him for the price of mandrakes. What Jacob made of this information no one knows. But Leah went on to have another son, named Issachar, which meant "the reward of hire." She had a sixth son, named Zebulun, which meant "gifts." Last, she had a daughter named Dinah.

Finally, God heard the suffering Rachel—as though remembering a lost child. God blessed Rachel so that in due time she gave birth to a

Jacob had a large family. His beloved wife Rachel gave him two sons. His sad wife Leah gave him six sons and a daughter. His wife Bilhah, handmaid of Rachel, gave him two sons. His wife Zilpah, handmaid of Leah, gave him two sons.

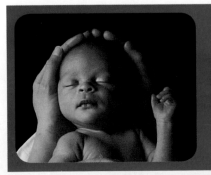

WHAT'S IN A NAME?
Naming children properly is important in many societies, but customs differ widely. Children are often named after another person (maybe an ancestor or hero figure), and can reflect gender, birth order, or day of the week the child was born, among other things. Sometimes names can have meaning significant to the parents in ways similar to the names in these biblical stories, names that range from connotational and emotive (such as "laughter") to ideas about the construction of identity (such as "rich," "beautiful," "farmer," "strong warrior").

son. She called him Joseph, which meant "my shame is removed" and "may there be another son."

By this point, Jacob had served Laban seven years for Leah, then seven years for Rachel, and finally six additional years for herds of animals. It was time to return to Canaan. Jacob gathered his four wives, eleven sons, one daughter, servants, and hundreds of camels, donkeys, oxen, sheep, and goats. They retraced the steps Jacob had taken 20 years before. When they arrived at the sacred spot where Jacob had dreamed of the heavenward ladder, task messengers met them. Jacob stopped and sent ahead servants with animals as gifts for his estranged brother Esau. Jacob longed for peace with him.

Then he heard Esau was coming to meet him, bringing an army. In fear, Jacob sent his family across the Jabbok Ford. He waited alone on the near side of the ford for whatever would come that night. An unknown man appeared—an apparition? A task messenger? They wrestled. Jacob's hip got dislocated. He cried, "Let me go. Dawn comes. Bless me." The man asked, "Who are you?" When Jacob told him, the man renamed him Israel, which meant "he struggled with a divine being and prevailed"—just as God had renamed Abram as Abraham. The man blessed Jacob.

The man never said his own name. But that man had blessed Jacob-Israel, just as a task messenger would have; so Jacob-Israel named that place Peniel, which meant "I have seen God face-to-face and survived."

Israel limped away—his thigh painful. To this day, the Children of Israel are prohibited from eating thigh meat.

As Israel continued traveling southward, Esau and his men arrived. Israel arranged his servants and family in order, with Rachel and their son Joseph, the favored ones, in the last and most protected position. He went to Esau, bowing seven times. When the long-lost brothers saw one another, they hugged. Esau refused the gifts. He had wives and children, land and animals, enough wealth of his own. But Israel said that seeing Esau was like seeing the face of God. So Esau accepted the gifts.

Finally, the newly remade Jacob, who had been born holding on to his brother's heel, who had tricked that brother twice, now deserved his new name of Israel. He no longer clung to anyone, he no longer needed tricks.

Esau had changed, too. As a young man he could never do anything right. Now he was a rich man with a large family.

The brothers left—Israel to the land he had grown up in and Esau to the home he had made in Seir—at peace with each other. That's what mattered. Israel's long journey, his penance, had been rewarded.

Along the final stretch of the road homeward, Israel's beloved wife Rachel gave birth to a second son. But she was old and labor was harsh. As her energies faded, Rachel named the boy Ben-Oni, which meant "son of my suffering." She died. Israel buried her in that place, which was called Bethlehem.

He renamed the boy Benjamin. So Abram and his wife Sarai, their grandson Jacob, and now Jacob's son Ben-Oni, had all been renamed. But this time it was the father, not God, who did it, for Benjamin meant "son of the right hand." Being Rachel's child, his father favored him. In all, Israel had 12 sons now, and his daughter Dinah.

Jacob wrestled with a stranger in the night. He was injured, but he prevailed, and the mysterious stranger blessed him and renamed him Israel.

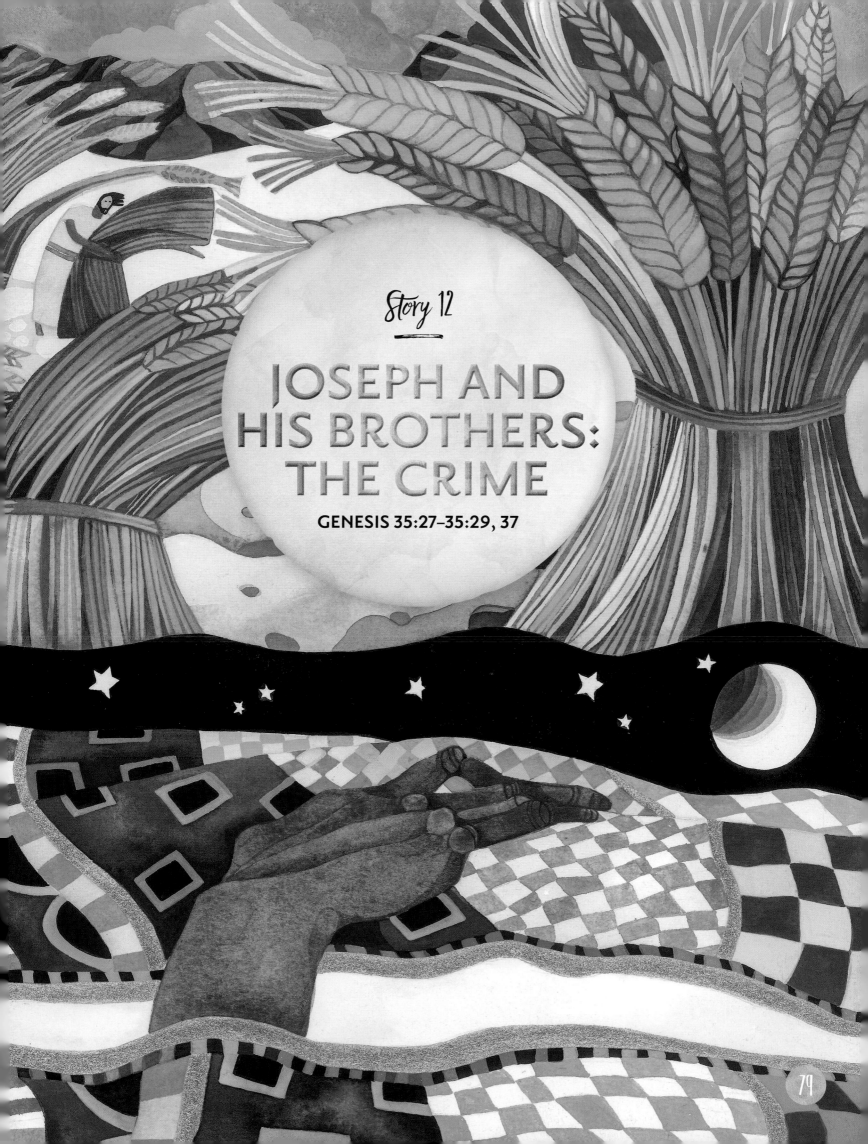

Story 12

JOSEPH AND HIS BROTHERS: THE CRIME

GENESIS 35:27–35:29, 37

JOSEPH AND HIS BROTHERS: THE CRIME

Isaac died of old age. His firstborn, Esau, and his second-born, Israel, united to bury him, just as Abraham's firstborn, Ishmael, and second-born, Isaac, had united to bury him. Abraham's offspring understood the importance of family, though it seemed that importance needed to be learned over and over again, with each new generation.

In the present generation stood the 12 sons of Israel. The baby Benjamin did hardly anything with the older ones. But the 11 others worked together in the fields, tending the flocks. Now Joseph, the son of Israel's favorite wife, Rachel, was his father's favorite son—not counting the baby Benjamin. And Joseph knew it. He tattletaled to his father about his brothers' shenanigans. It wasn't hard to do—for his brothers could behave like violent toughs and bumblers.

Israel made his favored son Joseph a tunic as ornamented and beautiful as any woman's festive dress. Joseph's brothers were consumed with jealousy and treated him spitefully. Then Joseph made things worse for himself ... much worse; he foolishly revealed dreams he was having.

His father, Israel, when he was still named Jacob, had had that amazing dream of a ladder that extended toward the heavens. Now it was Joseph's turn to dream. And he told his brothers all about his first dream. In the dream the brothers were binding sheaves in the field, when Joseph's sheaf suddenly stood tall and the sheaves of his brothers gathered around and bowed to it. The brothers were aghast at what this dream might mean. And they hated Joseph. "Do you plan to reign over us?" Then Joseph, who might not have been the most thoughtful of fellows, had another dream and again told it in full to his brothers and his father. In this dream the sun and moon and 11 stars bowed to him.

Previous: Joseph, Israel's favorite son, had a dream in which he and his brothers were binding sheaves of grain in the field. In the dream, Joseph's sheaf stood tall and all the other sheaves bowed down to it.

Israel was annoyed. "Shall we really come and bow down to you—your mother and I and all your brothers?" So the brothers hated Joseph even more, and his father kept all of this in mind.

One day the brothers went out together to a pasture very far away without Joseph. Israel told Joseph to go join his brothers. Was this some kind of trick Israel was playing on Joseph? He knew very well how his older sons felt toward this younger son. And by this point, Joseph knew, too. But Joseph was his father's obedient son. He said, "Here I am," just as Abraham had responded to God when he was told to sacrifice Isaac, just as both Esau and Jacob had responded to their father Isaac when he was bedridden and calling to them. Those words preceded pain. Was Joseph aware he was in mortal danger?

Joseph had a second dream, in which the sun and the moon and 11 stars all bowed down to him. This made Israel and Joseph's brothers believe that Joseph thought he should rule over his parents and his 11 brothers.

Aware or not, Joseph went in search of his brothers, who spied him coming from afar. After all, that colorful tunic was unmistakable. And they plotted to kill him, throw him in a pit, and tell their father, Israel, that a vicious beast had devoured him. Only Reuben, the very first of Israel's sons, stood up for him. He said they should throw Joseph in the pit alive, and he secretly planned to come back and save his younger brother.

When Joseph arrived, the brothers stripped off his coat—that source of envy—and flung him into the pit without even any water to drink. Then they sat down to eat—the thought of murdering their younger brother had no effect on their appetite! That's when they lifted their eyes—just as Hagar had lifted her eyes when she thought her son Ishmael was about to die of thirst in the wilderness and just as Abraham had lifted his eyes before he was about to sacrifice Isaac. This lifting of the eyes brought the brothers an answer different from murder: a caravan of Ishmaelites traveling with gum and balm and ladanum piled high on their camels. Judah, Leah's fourth son, said they should sell Joseph to these wanderers, and that way keep their hands clean of their brother's blood.

For 20 pieces of silver, they sold Joseph.

The brothers killed a kid goat and smeared his blood on Joseph's tunic, then brought it home to Israel. "Is this Joseph's?" they asked, knowing full well it was. Keening and rending his clothes, Israel mourned for his favorite son that a savage beast had surely killed. He would not be consoled. Did he understand that he'd set up this murder? Or did he maybe know somehow deep inside that Joseph still lived, but was lost to him?

CARAVAN TRADE
Joseph was sold to a caravan of Ishmaelites—descendants of Abraham's older son Ishmael, who had produced his own 12 tribes. The Ishmaelites were herders and merchants, with villages and trade routes from Egypt to Syria. They traded cosmetics, perfumes, medicines. The caravan mentioned in this story carries three medicinal drugs. Gum was made from mixing dried sap with water to form a soothing gel for burns, cough, and digestive problems. Balm, a fragrant tree resin, healed wounds. Ladanum, a milky tincture from certain poppy plants, was a painkiller.

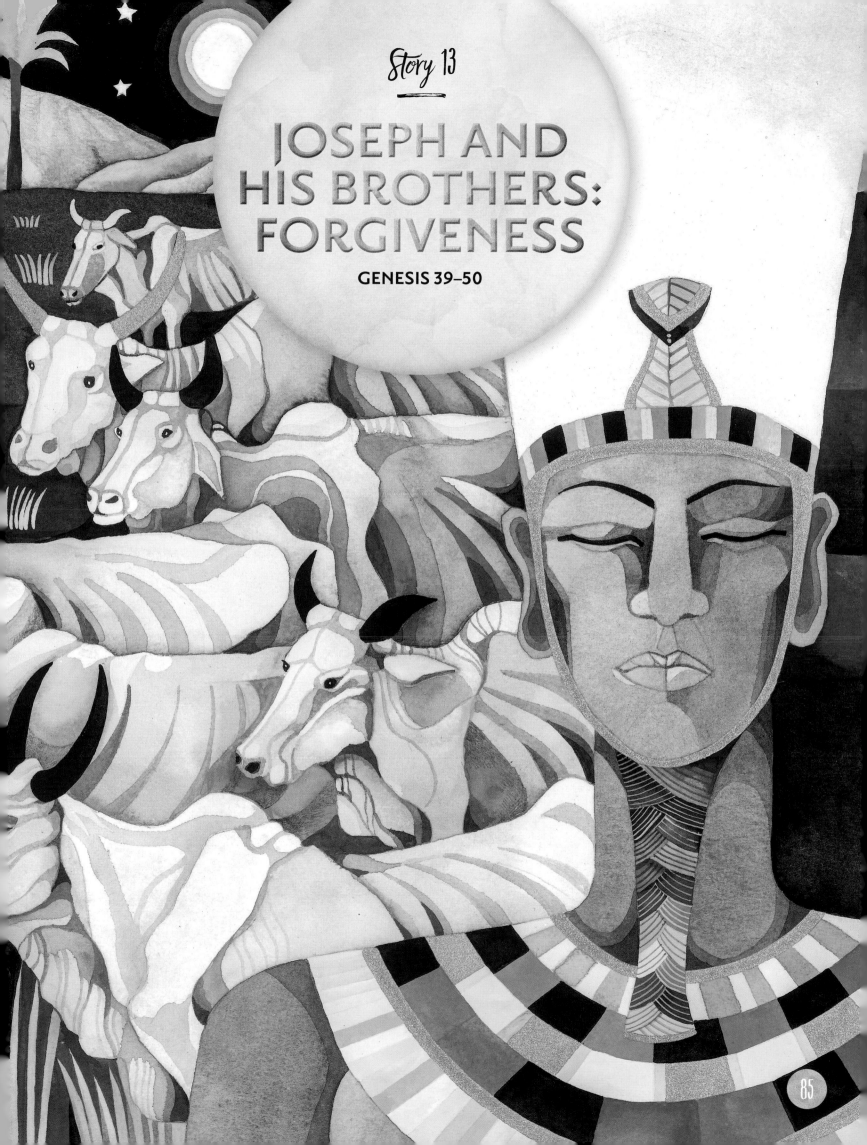

JOSEPH AND HIS BROTHERS: FORGIVENESS

Meanwhile, the Ishmaelites traveled to Egypt and sold Joseph to Potifar, adviser to Pharaoh, ruler of Egypt. The Lord made everything Joseph did turn out right. Soon Potifar put Joseph in charge, while he spent his day eating.

All was well. For a while. Then Potifar's wife noticed how handsome Joseph was. She wanted romance.

Joseph couldn't betray Potifar or God. Day after day, the woman persisted and Joseph refused. Finally, she seized him by his shirt. He escaped, without his shirt. The woman ran outside and accused Joseph of assaulting her. She identified him as a Hebrew—that word that meant he was an outsider. When Potifar heard, he imprisoned Joseph.

Again the Lord made everything Joseph did turn out right; the prison warden put Joseph in charge. Two new prisoners arrived, the cupbearer and the baker of Pharaoh. Each had a dream no one could interpret. Well, Joseph could interpret dreams!

The cupbearer said, "In my dream a vine with three tendrils budded and made grapes. I squashed them in Pharaoh's cup and handed it to him."

Joseph quickly said the tendrils were days. "In three days Pharaoh will pardon you. You'll be his cupbearer. When you get out, tell Pharaoh of me. I was stolen from the Hebrews."

Now the baker spoke. "In my dream I carried three baskets on my head. Birds pecked at the bread in the top one."

Joseph answered quickly again. "In three days Pharaoh will slice off your head and put it on a pole, where birds will peck it."

It happened just like that.

But the cupbearer forgot and never spoke a word of Joseph to

Previous: Pharaoh dreamed that seven fat cows appeared in the River Nile. Then seven bony cows appeared and ate them up. What could it mean? He needed a dream interpreter—he needed Joseph.

Pharaoh. Two years passed. Then Pharaoh himself had dreams. He dreamed seven fat cows emerged from the River Nile. Seven bony cows emerged and devoured the fat cows. Pharaoh awoke with a start. Then he slept and dreamed again. A single stalk sprouted with seven juicy ears of corn. Another stalk sprouted with seven dry ears that gobbled up the juicy ears. The pounding of his heart woke Pharaoh. He called soothsayers, but none could interpret his dream. That's when the cup-bearer remembered Joseph.

So Pharaoh summoned Joseph. Joseph said the two dreams were but one. God was warning Pharaoh of the future. Seven years of plenty—like seven fat cows and seven juicy ears of corn—would be followed by seven years of famine—like seven bony cows and seven dry ears of corn. Pharaoh should hire a wise man to collect excess food during the years of plenty and store it for the years of famine.

Pharaoh chose Joseph as that wise man. He gave Joseph his signet ring, fine linen clothes, a gold necklace. He had him ride in the royal chariot. He gave him Asenat, daughter of Potifar, as his wife.

A baker who was imprisoned dreamed that he balanced three baskets of bread on his head and birds pecked at the ones on top.

For seven years Egypt was bountiful. Joseph collected food as his family grew. He had two sons, Manasseh and Ephraim. Then seven years of famine began. But Egypt survived, because of the storehouses of provision.

No other lands had a wise man collecting provisions through the fat years. So when famine came, people outside Egypt suffered. In Canaan, Joseph's father, Israel, kept Benjamin, the youngest, at his side, but sent all 10 of his other sons to Egypt to trade silver for food.

The brothers came before Joseph and saw a fine man, the vizier to Pharaoh, speaking Egyptian and conversing with them through an interpreter. They didn't recognize their brother. But Joseph knew them; they bowed to him, like in his first dream. He pretended to think they were spies. They protested; they were sons of a man living in Canaan, who had stayed behind with their youngest brother. One other brother was "no more." They had come purely from hunger.

Now that youngest brother was Benjamin, Joseph's only full brother. How Joseph must have longed to know him again. Joseph threw his brothers in prison for three days. Then they could go home with food, but one must stay until the others returned, bringing their youngest brother.

The brothers talked among themselves. Reuben scolded them, saying they never should have harmed their brother Joseph. He said they deserved this present situation for being heartless.

Joseph understood them, though they didn't know it. He turned his back and wept; brothers are brothers—and forgiveness comes when repentance is sincere. Still, he detained his brother Simeon and sent the others home with food. And he had the silver they had paid put back in their bags.

When the brothers discovered silver in their bags, they figured God had tricked them. Now that Egyptian vizier would think they were thieves. They told Israel everything. Israel refused to let Benjamin go to Egypt. "My son will not go. His brother is dead and he is all that remains. If harm should come to him, I would die of sorrow." What a terrible thing for the brothers to hear. They were Israel's children, too.

Time passed, with Simeon languishing in prison and the people of Canaan going hungry again. Finally, Israel told the brothers to return to Egypt for food. The brothers said there was no point going without Benjamin. Judah vowed to protect Benjamin—otherwise they would all die of hunger.

Israel finally let all his sons go, with the silver from last time plus double that amount for this time, and all Canaan's best honey, gum, ladanum, pistachios, and almonds. When they got to Egypt, Joseph ordered a feast for the visitors.

That night the brothers bowed to Joseph. "How is your father?" Joseph asked.

"Alive and well," they answered.

"Is this your youngest brother?" Without waiting for an answer, Joseph added, "God be gracious to you." He quickly went into another room and wept. When he returned, they prepared to eat—but Joseph sat separately because Egyptians did not eat with Hebrews. The brothers took their assigned seats—which were in the order of their birth. They were astonished. Who knew that order? And somehow Benjamin wound up with five times the portion of the others. It was as though he was the favored baby here, just as he was at home. How could this Egyptian nobleman know?

In the morning, Joseph let his brothers head homeward, their bags full of food. But he also had their silver tucked into their bags and, in Benjamin's bag, Joseph had his own goblet tucked as well. When the men were a short distance away, Joseph's servants overcame them

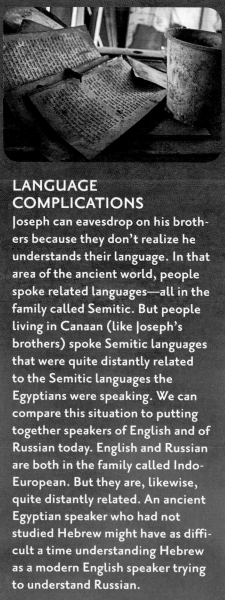

LANGUAGE COMPLICATIONS

Joseph can eavesdrop on his brothers because they don't realize he understands their language. In that area of the ancient world, people spoke related languages—all in the family called Semitic. But people living in Canaan (like Joseph's brothers) spoke Semitic languages that were quite distantly related to the Semitic languages the Egyptians were speaking. We can compare this situation to putting together speakers of English and of Russian today. English and Russian are both in the family called Indo-European. But they are, likewise, quite distantly related. An ancient Egyptian speaker who had not studied Hebrew might have as difficult a time understanding Hebrew as a modern English speaker trying to understand Russian.

and accused them of having stolen their master's goblet. The servants said the thief would have to stay in Egypt. And, of course, they found the goblet in Benjamin's bag.

The brothers were distraught. They returned to Joseph's house and threw themselves on the ground. They offered to stay as servants. But Joseph insisted that only Benjamin stay. That's when Judah opened his heart. He described how their father doted on Benjamin. Benjamin was all that remained of his dear wife Rachel. Should Benjamin not return to his father, the old man would die.

That admission must have rent Judah's soul—and the souls of the other brothers.

Judah begged the vizier to accept him as a servant, and let the rest of them go home.

Joseph's heart opened now, too. He wept and told them he was their brother Joseph. They were dumbfounded. But Joseph told them not to regret anything. All of this was God's plan. For look—as vizier, Joseph had collected food and was helping people everywhere survive this famine. Surely, that was good. But only two years of famine had passed. For

the next five, Israel and his sons and their families should move to Egypt.

Pharaoh agreed: He promised them the best soil, in the part of Egypt called Goshen.

That's what they did—moved en masse in their wagons. Israel couldn't wait to see Joseph again. Yet he was filled with trepidation; Egypt was not home. But God called to him, and Israel responded, "Here I am." God told him his offspring would form a great nation in Egypt.

When they arrived, Joseph wept on his father's neck. Israel's offspring became herders in Goshen. The famine was bitter, but all survived. In fact, they thrived, so they stayed on in Goshen. After 17 years, Israel became ill. He blessed his sons, so that each of the 12 would head a tribe that would multiply and thrive.

When Israel died, Egypt mourned for 70 days. Israel's sons brought his body to the cave in his homeland where Abraham, Sarah, Isaac, and Rebekah were buried. Only Rachel, who had died while traveling, wasn't there.

The brothers and their families returned to Goshen. After all, Egypt was their home. For the time being.

Joseph hid a goblet in his little brother Benjamin's bag. Then he had his servants accuse the brothers of being thieves, so they had to stay in Egypt. When the brothers stood again in front of Joseph, he revealed who he was and told them to come with their father, Israel, to live in Egypt while the famine lasted.

Story 14

THE BABY MOSES

EXODUS 1–2

THE BABY MOSES

THE NILE
The Nile River and the Amazon River vie for the title of longest river in the world. The Nile River flows northwest over 4,000 miles (6,437 km) to empty into the Mediterranean Sea. It was the main highway through Egypt, deep, wide, and fast, with crocodiles and hippos living along and in it, and flocks of herons and pelicans relying on it. Since the Nile overflowed its banks every summer, the mud left behind was wonderfully fertile for growing crops. Today the river has many slow, marshy areas. But we know marshes were abundant in ancient times, too, since the ancient symbol of Lower Egypt was the papyrus (a source of paper), while the ancient symbol for Upper Egypt was the lotus, both water plants that grow in mud submerged in shallow water.

The 12 sons of Israel lived in Egypt in the land called Goshen: Reuben, Simeon, Levi, Judah, Dan, Naphtali, Gad, Asher, Issachar, Zebulun, Joseph, and Benjamin.

These Children of Israel, as they were known—the sons and their families—numbered 70 people. As the years passed, more offspring came. The original 12 brothers died, but their offspring prospered.

Pharaoh also died. Then came a pharaoh who had never known Joseph. He looked around and saw the numerous Children of Israel. He told his people that the nation of the Children of Israel was a threat to Egypt and must be crushed. That made the Egyptians glare at the Children of Israel with fear and loathing. They assigned them the hardest labor, building with mortar and bricks in town and doing every kind of task in the field.

Still, the Children of Israel thrived. So Pharaoh told the Hebrew midwives to kill newborn boys. In horror, the midwives disobeyed. They told Pharaoh that Hebrew women were so hardy, they gave birth on their own; they were already nursing their sons by the time the midwives arrived. Thwarted, Pharaoh ordered newborn Hebrew boys be thrown into the River Nile.

Disaster had come.

A man in the household of Levi already had a daughter and a little son. The next child, however, was another boy—oh no! By law, he would be thrown into the Nile. The wife kept the babe close for three months, but it was impossible to hide him longer. She made a wicker basket watertight with pitch, just like the giant ark that Noah had made, and set the child in it. She hid the basket in reeds along the riverbank. What could she

have been thinking? Crocodiles haunted the river. Hippos tipped over boats. So many dangers! But desperate times could make one rash. The babe's sister watched from a safe distance, to see what would happen next.

Pharaoh's daughter and her maidens came to bathe in the river. She saw the basket and made a handmaid fetch it. When she heard the babe's cries and gazed at his face, she knew he was a Hebrew. She pitied him.

The babe's big sister proved herself clever. She came to Pharaoh's daughter and offered to summon a wet nurse from the Hebrews to suckle the babe. Then she brought back her mother. Pharaoh's daughter said to the woman, "Care for this child until he is weaned. I will pay you well for this." The babe's mother got to take her dear boy home again. When he was weaned, she brought him back to Pharaoh's daughter.

Pharaoh's daughter treated the boy like a son. She named him Moses, which meant "out of the water." Moses knew that the Children of Israel were his kinsmen and he was curious. When Moses was a young man, he went to visit those kinsmen to know more about who he truly

Pharaoh's daughter found a basket among the reeds of the River Nile. Inside was a tiny babe—a Hebrew, for sure. Her heart opened. She would save this boy.

was. He saw an Egyptian man beating a man he identified as a Hebrew. Moses couldn't bear unfairness. He looked around—not a witness in sight. So he struck down the Egyptian and buried his body.

The next day Moses came across two Hebrews brawling. He broke up the fight. One of the men asked, "Who are you to act as ruler? Do you plan to kill me like you killed that Egyptian?" So Moses had been mistaken; there were witnesses to his crime. Soon Pharaoh learned of his crime, and Moses had to flee.

He went to far-off Midian and rested by a well. Ah, another well. A well had appeared before Hagar when she needed to save her son Ishmael in the desert. When Israel—then known as Jacob—had gone to seek his uncle Laban to escape the wrath of Esau, he saw Rachel coming to water her sheep at a well. Wells meant salvation and love for Hagar and Jacob-Israel.

This well meant the same for Moses. Soon after Moses arrived, along came seven daughters of a priest, to draw water for their father's flock. Other shepherds bullied the girls and drove them off so they could serve their own flocks first. Moses played hero; he watered the girls' flocks. The girls told their father Jethro that an Egyptian man had rescued them and watered the flocks. Jethro made his daughters bring Moses to him for a meal. The next thing Moses knew, he was living with them. He took the daughter Zipporah as his wife. They had a son named Gershom.

Years passed and Pharaoh died. But the next pharaoh was even harsher toward the Children of Israel. And finally God remembered the covenant with Abraham, whereby Abraham's descendants would place their trust in God and God would watch over them. The Children of Israel had lived in Egypt 430 years. God knew it was time to bring these people home.

Moses' mother had to give him up when he was older. She brought him to the daughter of Pharaoh, who raised him as though he were her own.

THE TEN PLAGUES

Moses was tending sheep in the wilderness when he wandered to the mountain of God called Horeb. A bush was on fire! Yet the fire didn't consume it. He turned to look attentively. The Lord noticed that look. "Moses, Moses." That voice seemed to come from the burning bush.

"Here I am."

God told Moses to take off his sandals; this was holy ground. The Lord said the pain of the Children of Israel must stop. They must go to a land flowing with milk and honey. The Lord instructed Moses to tell Pharaoh the Children of Israel should leave.

A land flowing with milk and honey? Egypt was not good grazing land—so milk was scarce. Rain was, too. To water the crops, you had to stomp in the mud to form irrigation troughs that trapped the river's overflow in flooding season. In this new land, instead of beating the earth for water, you could look up to the rains from heaven. And honey! Oh, the tales the Children of Israel told of old days in the homeland when people made date honey. Moses drooled.

Still, he was afraid of Pharaoh. "Who am I to speak to Pharaoh?"

God answered, "I will be with you."

But Moses said, "I can't just say our God gave me orders. People will want to know your name. Who are you?"

God said, "I am what I am. I am the Lord, God of your fathers."

God told Moses to prepare the Children of Israel. Pharaoh would resist at first, but in the end, he would let them go. With riches.

"No one will believe me," said Moses. After all, he was new in this community.

"What's that in your hand?" said the Lord.

"A staff."

"Throw it on the ground."

Moses flung the staff. It became a serpent.

Previous: Moses had become a simple shepherd when God appeared to him in the form of a burning bush that told him it was time to lead the Children of Israel out of Egypt and home again, to the old country.

God gave Moses signs that he could show the Children of Israel and Pharaoh, so they would believe him. The first sign was this: Moses threw his staff on the ground and it turned into a serpent.

"Grab its tail."

Moses forced himself to. The serpent turned into his staff again.

"Put your hand inside your shirt."

Moses did. His hand came out dead white.

"Put it back in your shirt."

Moses did. His hand came out healthy again.

"If they don't believe the first sign, they will believe the second. If not, throw water from the Nile on the ground. It will turn to blood. They will believe this, the third sign."

Moses knew the river was tainted with the blood of slain boys, babies from the Children of Israel whose death Pharaoh had ordered. Still, he didn't want this task. His mouth felt heavy, his tongue fat. "I'm not a man of words."

"Who makes one mute or deaf or sighted or blind? Me. I will be your mouth."

Moses' knees shook. "Please, send someone else."

"All right!" said the Lord in annoyance. "In Egypt you have an older brother Aaron. He can speak for you. I will speak through you both."

Moses took his wife and sons on donkeys to Egypt. Just then, Aaron came along. Moses explained everything to him, then Aaron explained everything to the Children of Israel. Moses performed the three signs; the Children of Israel believed them.

But the Lord warned Moses that Pharaoh would resist. Indeed, the Lord would strengthen Pharaoh's heart against Moses. Moses didn't ask why. But he was soon to learn.

Moses and Aaron told Pharaoh that the Children of Israel needed to leave Egypt for three days to worship God.

Pharaoh refused. He needed the Children of Israel for labor. He now made their labor even harsher. Instead of supplying straw to add

to the mud as they made bricks, from now on they'd have to gather straw for themselves and still make the same number of bricks daily.

The Children of Israel complained. Pharaoh said they were shirkers. They turned on Moses and Aaron. Moses appealed to the Lord. The Lord said, "Now you will see what I will do to Pharaoh. He will end up driving away the Children of Israel."

Moses and Aaron went back to Pharaoh and said they were messengers of God.

"Show me proof."

Aaron threw the staff on the ground; it turned into a serpent.

Pharaoh called his magicians and had them do the same with their staffs. The ground writhed with serpents. Aaron's serpent swallowed the others.

Pharaoh didn't flinch. His heart strengthened; the Children of Israel could not leave.

Moses brought the first plague. He struck the water of the River Nile with his staff. It turned to blood. The fish died. A stink hovered everywhere. The people had to dig wells for drinking water.

Moses brought plague after plague: a bloody river with dead fish, a swarm of frogs, lice, wild animals, a disease among the livestock, a cloud of burning ash, a hailstorm.

After seven days, the water cleared and Moses asked Pharaoh again. When Pharaoh refused, Aaron brought the second plague. Aaron held his staff over rivers and ponds; frogs came. They hopped into bedrooms, ovens, kneading bowls. Pharaoh thought it was nothing more than froggy magic. He had his magicians make frogs appear, too. But Pharaoh needed the frogs to leave, so he told Moses to get his god to take away the frogs. In return he would let the Children of Israel leave.

The frogs died, except those in the river. Their bodies were heaped high. The land reeked of death stench.

Pharaoh strengthened his heart; he changed his mind.

Aaron brought the third plague. His staff struck the dust. Lice surged everywhere. Pharaoh called his magicians so they could meet magic with magic. The magicians failed. They said, "This is the finger of God," for they recognized what Pharaoh couldn't. Pharaoh's heart strengthened again.

The fourth plague came. A horde of wild creatures entered houses and raced through fields, leaving ruination. Only the land of Goshen, where the Children of Israel lived, was spared. Pharaoh relented. "Go. But don't leave Egypt." Moses pleaded: The Children of Israel needed to sacrifice sheep to the Lord. Egyptians didn't allow such things. They would stone them. At that moment, Pharaoh agreed. "But don't go far." The Lord made the horde of wild creatures go away. Then, of course, Pharaoh strengthened his heart and changed his mind, so the Children of Israel could not leave, after all.

The fifth plague came. A disease afflicted livestock—donkeys, camels, cattle, sheep. They died. But the livestock of the Children of Israel stayed strong. Pharaoh saw and still the Children of Israel could not go.

Moses and Aaron brought the sixth plague. Moses threw handfuls of kiln soot into the air; it coated everything and everyone, until their skin broke out in burning boils. Even the magicians were stricken till they could not stand. Yet the Lord strengthened Pharaoh's heart. The Lord had motives that no one understood … not yet.

The Lord had Moses warn Pharaoh of the seventh plague if Pharaoh continued to refuse to let the Children of Israel go. Hail would fall, unrelenting. Those Egyptians who believed Moses brought households and cattle indoors. The others didn't. Moses stretched his staff heavenward; hail came in balls of ice and fire, with deafening thunder. People and animals, grass and trees, the budding barley and flax—all were smashed, except in the land of Goshen. Pharaoh was appalled. "The Lord is right. Egypt is wrong." He promised to let the Children of Israel go if the hail stopped. Moses

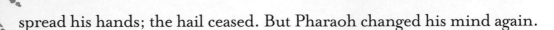

spread his hands; the hail ceased. But Pharaoh changed his mind again.

The Lord was not yet done toying with the Egyptians. They had to learn that it wasn't magic that mattered; it was humans' relationship with God.

Moses and Aaron brought the eighth plague. Locusts swarmed the land so thick people couldn't see the dirt. Locusts ate the stubble that remained of the broken crops. They sullied homes. The Egyptians told Pharaoh to stop this nonsense.

Pharaoh said to Moses, "Go." Then he frowned and asked, "Who exactly will go?"

"Old and young, men and women, cattle and sheep."

Pharaoh would allow only the men to go. That's who was needed for worship.

Though this was not what Moses had asked for, it was a start. So Moses stretched out his staff; winds blew away the locusts. But when Pharaoh didn't relent, Moses brought the ninth plague. He held his staff heavenward and darkness fell, heavy and palpable, like before creation. For three days no colors showed, no person could detect any other by sight. Only in Goshen were homes filled with light.

Pharaoh called Moses. "Go. Take your families. But leave behind sheep and cattle."

"We need our livestock," said Moses. Without them, how could they make sacrifices to the Lord?

"Go. Don't see my face again. If you do, you will die."

"I will never see your face again."

Pharaoh was left with his mistake solid in his heart. So the tenth plague had to come. A monster of a plague. But first, God wanted the Children of Israel to prepare for travel.

The Lord told Moses that this new moon was a new beginning. From now on this month would start the year for the

FOOD AND FASTING
In this tale we see the origin of the requirement that Jews eat unleavened bread (matzo) during the celebration of Passover. Many religions require special eating habits during celebrations, including fasting, and many have dietary restrictions year-round. Often those restrictions involve whether or not you can eat animals, and, if so, which ones. For example, Buddhism promotes a vegetarian diet; Islam prohibits pork and certain birds; Hinduism prohibits beef and promotes a vegetarian diet; Judaism prohibits pork, shellfish, and certain other sea creatures; and Greek Orthodox Christianity has so many fasting days when meat, dairy products, and eggs are prohibited that they are vegetarians for more than half the year. Studies suggest such dietary restrictions have health benefits.

Children of Israel. On the 10th day of that first month, a lamb should be chosen by every large household or by groups of smaller households. These lambs should be tended for four days. At twilight on the 14th of the month—under full moon—the lambs should be roasted. The Children of Israel should smear lamb blood on their doorposts and door lintels. They should eat that meat with unleavened bread and bitter herbs. The meat must be dry roasted; leftovers must be burned at dawn. As the people ate, they had to tie their cloaks up around their loins, wear their sandals, and hold their staffs; they had to eat fast, ready for travel. The Lord told what terrible things would happen to the Egyptians as the Children of Israel ate. Every year the Children of Israel would remember this night by eating unleavened bread. For seven days they would tell tales of their suffering and salvation.

On the 10th day the Children of Israel chose the lambs, watched over them for four days, then roasted them.

At midnight of that 14th night, as the Children of Israel were roasting the lambs, the Lord killed the firstborn in every Egyptian family—humans and beasts. But the Lord passed over homes smeared with lamb blood on the doorposts.

Across Egypt, parents, including Pharaoh, woke to find their first-born dead. Their cries could have broken the strongest heart. Pharaoh told Moses and Aaron to leave—never come back. The Egyptians pushed on them silver and gold ornaments, as payment to end this scourge.

The Children of Israel left. Others joined them—a motley group of travelers—600,000 strong. Moses brought the bones of his ancestor Joseph, to return them to the homeland.

The Lord guided them, appearing as a pillar of cloud by day, a pillar of fire by night. For seven days the Children of Israel ate unleavened bread and told tales of how the Lord had passed over their homes. The retelling of the story sealed it in their memories.

Locusts and darkness came as the eighth and ninth plagues. But the 10th plague was the worst. As the Children of Israel roasted lamb to eat before their journey, the Lord killed the firstborn in every Egyptian family.

Story 16

THE REED SEA AND MANNA

EXODUS 14–16

THE REED SEA AND MANNA

The Lord strengthened Pharaoh's heart yet again, for Pharaoh needed one more lesson. Really? After all that the Egyptians and the Children of Israel had suffered? Yet the Lord wanted to ensure for all time that no one doubt who was truly in charge. The Egyptians needed to understand divine omnipotence.

So Pharaoh changed his mind. What would Egypt do without Hebrews as a workforce, after all? He picked 600 chariots and many troops. Off they went, into the wilderness, after the wandering Children of Israel.

The Children of Israel arrived at the shore of the Reed Sea and knew not where to turn. The Egyptians were at their heels; the sea was deep and wide. They turned in desperate accusation against Moses. "Was it for want of graves in Egypt that you took us out?" Death in their homes in Egypt would have been preferable to death here.

Moses calmed them. The Lord would surely save them.

The humans' complaints annoyed the Lord. In exasperation, the Lord told Moses to hold his staff over the waters. The sea would part for the Children of Israel to cross through.

That night a pillar of fire and clouds reigned behind the Children of Israel, holding the Egyptians at bay. Moses stretched out his staff. A hot, dry wind arose from the desert. This east wind blew all night, gradually spreading the water into two parts until the seabed appeared in the middle. The Children of Israel crossed.

It was morning by now, and the Egyptians plunged forth. Chariots, riders, onto that dry seabed in pursuit of the Children of Israel. Once they were all between the two walls of water, the Lord told Moses, on the far shore, to stretch his hand over the sea.

Moses did.

The walls of water tumbled down, drowning the Egyptians.

Previous: The Children of Israel had to flee, but the Reed Sea stood in the way. Moses held up his staff and a dry wind blew hard and long and hot. It separated the waters so a path formed from one shore to the other.

As the Egyptians pursued the Children of Israel across the dry seabed, Moses spread out his hand from the far shore and the parted walls of water came crashing down, killing them all.

A terrible and terrifying end.

Yet now the Children of Israel were truly free. They celebrated by singing. The women danced, with jangling timbrels. Miriam, Aaron's and Moses' big sister, who was known as a prophetess, chanted,

Sing to the Lord, the expansive divinity.

Horse and rider, the Lord has hurled into the sea.

But troubles were far from over. The Children of Israel wandered three days without water. When they came across some, it was bitter. The people complained to Moses, who, as usual, complained in turn to the Lord. The Lord showed Moses a lone tree and told him to fling it into the bitter water to turn it sweet. Everyone drank. Then Moses led them onward to a place of 12 springs of water and 70 date palms. That's where they camped.

But when they left the place of 12 springs, they wandered in hunger. The people remembered the old days in Egypt as though they had been wonderful, with plentiful meat and bread. With melons and sweet, fresh cucumbers, with garlic and tangy, juicy onions. It was not a real memory, but it felt real. They said they should have stayed in Egypt—death by hard work there was preferable to death by famine here.

The Lord told Moses what would happen, and Moses told the people. That night flocks of quail covered the camp, so people had meat aplenty. In the morning, dew coated everything. When it lifted, there were fine, white flakes, like frost. The people asked, *"Man hu? What is it?"* They collected it, ground it, boiled it, and made it into cakes to feed their households, for this *man-hu*—what they came to call manna—was bread. The manna was white on the outside, like coriander seed; inside was the taste of wafer in honey, like the richest cream. Moses told them to take only what they needed for that day, since the Lord promised to rain down manna over and over. Some hoarded anyway. In the morning, the extra was rotten with worms. Moses was furious that they had so little faith. After that, they gathered only what they needed, and somehow, no matter how much or little they gathered, it always came out right: no extras, no paucity. Moses told them that on the sixth day, they should gather double, because the seventh day would be a day of rest, to celebrate one's faith. That was just as God had done after creation—work for six days, rest on the seventh. On the morning of the seventh day, the extra bread from that manna was still fresh, so they didn't go hungry. After that, every seventh day—the Sabbath—was a day free of toil.

The Children of Israel saved some manna in a jar, sealed for future generations to see and know what had happened in the wilderness.

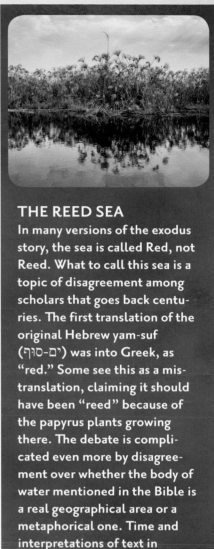

THE REED SEA
In many versions of the exodus story, the sea is called Red, not Reed. What to call this sea is a topic of disagreement among scholars that goes back centuries. The first translation of the original Hebrew yam-suf (יַם-סוּף) was into Greek, as "red." Some see this as a mistranslation, claiming it should have been "reed" because of the papyrus plants growing there. The debate is complicated even more by disagreement over whether the body of water mentioned in the Bible is a real geographical area or a metaphorical one. Time and interpretations of text in another language are always open to such debate, which makes works like the present one such a delightful challenge.

The Children of Israel celebrated their freedom from the Egyptians at last, with singing and dancing to the music of their timbrels.

THE TEN COMMANDMENTS AND THE LAWS

EXODUS 17–40,
DEUTERONOMY,
NUMBERS 13–14

THE TEN COMMANDMENTS AND THE LAWS

The desert was dry and hot. Everyone was parched. They complained. Moses feared they would stone him. The Lord told Moses to strike a rock in Horeb and water would shoot forth. Moses did. Everyone stopped arguing. That place was known after that as Massah and Meribah—Testing and Dispute.

After being in the wilderness three months, the Children of Israel arrived at the base of Mount Sinai. The Lord told Moses to prepare them to hear the covenant; the people washed their clothes and bodies. On the third day, thunder rumbled. Lightning split heavy clouds. A ram horn trumpeted louder and louder. Everyone trembled. The mountain burst into flame and quaked under a smoke blanket.

God then spoke the Ten Commandments.

I am the Lord. Worship only me.

Thou shalt not make images to worship.

Thou shalt not take my name in vain.

Honor the Sabbath.

Honor thy father and thy mother.

Thou shalt not murder.

Thou shalt be faithful to thy partner.

Thou shalt not steal.

Thou shalt not lie about thy neighbor.

Thou shalt not be covetous of what thy neighbor has.

The people saw lightning, fire, and smoke; they heard thunder; they were so afraid that they asked Moses to talk with God for them. Now that they knew God was real, they promised to follow whatever laws Moses brought them. The people stood far away while Moses went to the top of the mountain and stepped into the fog where God was.

Previous: While Moses had been busy up on Mount Sinai listening to God's laws, the Children of Israel made a golden calf. They danced around it and worshipped it, breaking one of the Ten Commandments.

God stated the many laws.

Laws about how to treat each other, the beasts, the land; how to care for life in a civilized society; how to treat strangers. Laws to protect servants, women, children. Laws to punish criminals but show mercy to those who err by accident. Laws that might be harsh but fair: a life for a life, an eye for an eye, a tooth for a tooth, a hand for a hand, a foot for a foot, a burn for a burn, a wound for a wound, a bruise for a bruise. Order and balance.

Laws about ritual: no magic, no witches. No curses against God. Never boil a kid goat in its mother's milk. The Sabbath must be a rest day for all, animals and servants included. Three times each year, all males must appear before God for festivals. In spring, the festival of flat bread, Passover. In summer, the festival of wheat-reaping. In autumn, the festival of the main harvest, at the turning of the year.

There were instructions on how to build a portable tabernacle, so the Lord could dwell among the people wherever they went. The tabernacle should be adorned with gold, silver, bronze. Curtains in indigo, purple, crimson. Panels of fine linen and goat hair, reddened ram skins and ocher-dyed skins. Lapis lazuli. A candelabra of gold with six shafts, each ending in a cup shaped like almond blossoms that must be filled with olive oil. The priests of this tabernacle, led by Aaron and his sons, must dress in sacred garments, filigreed with chains of gold, and wear breastplates with rows of precious stones: ruby, topaz, malachite, turquoise, sapphire, amethyst, jacinth, agate, crystal, beryl, carnelian, jasper. There should be an ark of acacia wood, overlaid with gold, with golden rings on the sides and feet for carrying poles to slide through, and a cover of gold decorated with hammered cherubim. Inside that ark Moses should place stone tablets that God had carved all these Commandments and laws onto.

The telling of these laws took a long time. The Children of Israel back at the foot of the mountain grew annoyed and doubtful. They asked Aaron to help them make gods to worship—false images that the Second Commandment ordered against. Aaron gathered their gold and made it into a molten calf. The next day, they prayed to the golden calf and celebrated.

Moses descended Mount Sinai with the two tablets. As he neared the camp, he saw the golden calf and the partying. His assistant Joshua warned him that things had gone astray. In anger, Moses smashed the tablets, burned up the golden calf, and demanded to know why Aaron had done such a thing. Aaron cowered and said the people scared him into it. Moses ordered the faithful to kill the others. Three thousand people died that day. Oh, woe! Moses acted as harsh as the harshest laws of God.

Moses now needed reassurance, through seeing the presence of God. God told Moses to stand in a cleft in a rock—a small cave—and when God passed by, Moses could see the wake of divine glory. Moses climbed upward. God came down in a cloud and revealed the glory of the Lord—loving, compassionate, constant, strict but fair. God told Moses to carve two more stone tablets, like the smashed ones. And God made another list of laws. Moses wrote them on the second set of tablets.

For 40 days and 40 nights Moses stayed with the Lord, writing. He did not eat or drink. When he descended the mountain with these tablets, his face glowed; he wore a veil to not frighten the people.

The people immediately set to work building the tabernacle.

More than a year after they'd left Egypt, the Lord told Moses to choose men, one from each of the 12 tribes of Israel, plus his assistant Joshua, who should go ahead to scout out the land of Canaan. For 40 days the scouts were gone. They returned with reports of a land flowing with milk and honey. The scouts brought good news in the form of gigantic fruits—pomegranates, dates, and a cluster of grapes so large it

Moses was so aghast at the people celebrating the golden calf that he smashed the tablets and ordered the faithful among his people to kill the others. His fury caused a slaughter.

THE NUMBER 40

The number 40 comes up repeatedly in the Bible. It is clearly associated in the stories up to now with the idea of trials or tests and of salvation and redemption. The rain poured 40 days and 40 nights in the Noah story. Moses lived 40 years in Egypt. He was on Mount Sinai for 40 days and nights. Moses sent scouts ahead for 40 days to investigate Canaan. The Children of Israel wandered 40 years in the desert. We will see this number in later stories, too. Many religions have specific numbers that are somehow significant, often magical. But 40 does not appear to be magical in Judaism; instead, it might simply stand for "many," and some scholars have noted that it is a natural number to choose for "many" since 40 years is about the span of a generation.

took two men to carry it on a pole. But they also brought bad news in the form of information—the people were gigantic. "We felt like grasshoppers in comparison." The Children of Israel wanted to return to Egypt. Only two scouts, Joshua and Caleb, believed that the Lord would protect them.

The Lord was enraged at the people's lack of faith. The Lord threatened to wipe them out with a plague—all but Moses' family—just as everyone had been wiped out in the time of Noah. Again, Moses argued: Others would hear of the death of the Children of Israel and think the Lord was powerless to save them. He reminded the Lord of past promises to be kind. The Lord relented. At a cost. The Children of Israel had to wander for years before they could enter the promised land. Wandering was harsh. Many died, including Miriam, sister to Moses and Aaron. Once again they ran out of water. Once again the Lord showed

Moses a rock and water gushed forth for people and livestock. Everyone was saved. Soon after, Aaron died. Everyone mourned for 30 days. The people complained. In fury, the Lord sent vipers. More died. Some ventured into the promised land before God allowed them, and died at enemy hands. There were little wars—skirmishes—and big wars—scourges.

As the time approached, Moses told the Children of Israel their history, from Abraham on. He repeated the laws and Commandments. He gave them courage to cross the River Jordan and claim the promised land, despite their fears of giant Canaanites. He called forth Joshua, his assistant, and lay his hands upon his head, giving him wisdom so Joshua could lead the people. Then, on the west side of the River Jordan, he died with a whisper from God. God buried him in Moab. Never again would there be a prophet like Moses who God knew face-to-face.

At this point, of the adults who had left Egypt, only two remained: Joshua and Caleb.

In all, the Children of Israel had wandered 40 years in the wilderness. They needed to go home; Joshua would finish the job.

Scouts brought back a cluster of huge grapes, with tales of gigantic people in Canaan. The Children of Israel were afraid. Plus, water was hard to come by. And then Aaron died. When the people complained, the Lord sent vipers. Moses, too, approached death. He passed on the job of leading the people home to Joshua.

JOSHUA AND THE BATTLE OF JERICHO

JOSHUA 1–8

JOSHUA AND THE BATTLE OF JERICHO

Joshua was Moses' young assistant. God had selected him to become the next leader. Moses had shared some of his spirit with him. Joshua had his own perspective on things: It wouldn't be easy to take over land in Canaan; people didn't surrender just like that. So Joshua sent two spies to scope out the land, particularly the city of Jericho.

The spies spent the night at the woman Rahab's house, which was built into the very wall of Jericho. The king heard and sent his men to capture them. Rahab said the spies had already left. She urged the king's men to pursue them. But, in fact, she had hidden the spies on her flat roof, among the flax stalks she slept on in the hottest weather. After the king's men left, Rahab explained to the spies why she had lied to her own people. "I know the Lord has promised you this land. We all know what happened at the Reed Sea. We quake in fear at you Children of Israel." She made the spies promise they would save her family when the Children of Israel entered the city. After all, they owed her. The spies told her to gather her parents, siblings, extended family, all within her home. She should hang a scarlet cord from her window.

The Children of Israel would see the cord and leave her clan undisturbed.

Rahab then lowered the spies out her window and told them to hide in the hills for three days.

The spies hid. When they finally returned to Joshua's camp, they told him the lay of the land. The Children of Israel prepared to enter Jericho, across the River Jordan. The priests led the way, carrying the golden ark with the covenant—the tablets of laws. Behind them came Joshua with 12 men, one from each tribe of Israel.

When they got to the river, Joshua told the priests to step in; the

Previous: The priests carried the golden ark with the tablets of law. When they came to the River Jordan, the water stopped rushing and rose up, leaving a dry river-bed. The priests walked across easily to the other shore.

A man from each of the 12 tribes of Israel picked up a large rock from the riverbed to bring to Gilgal.

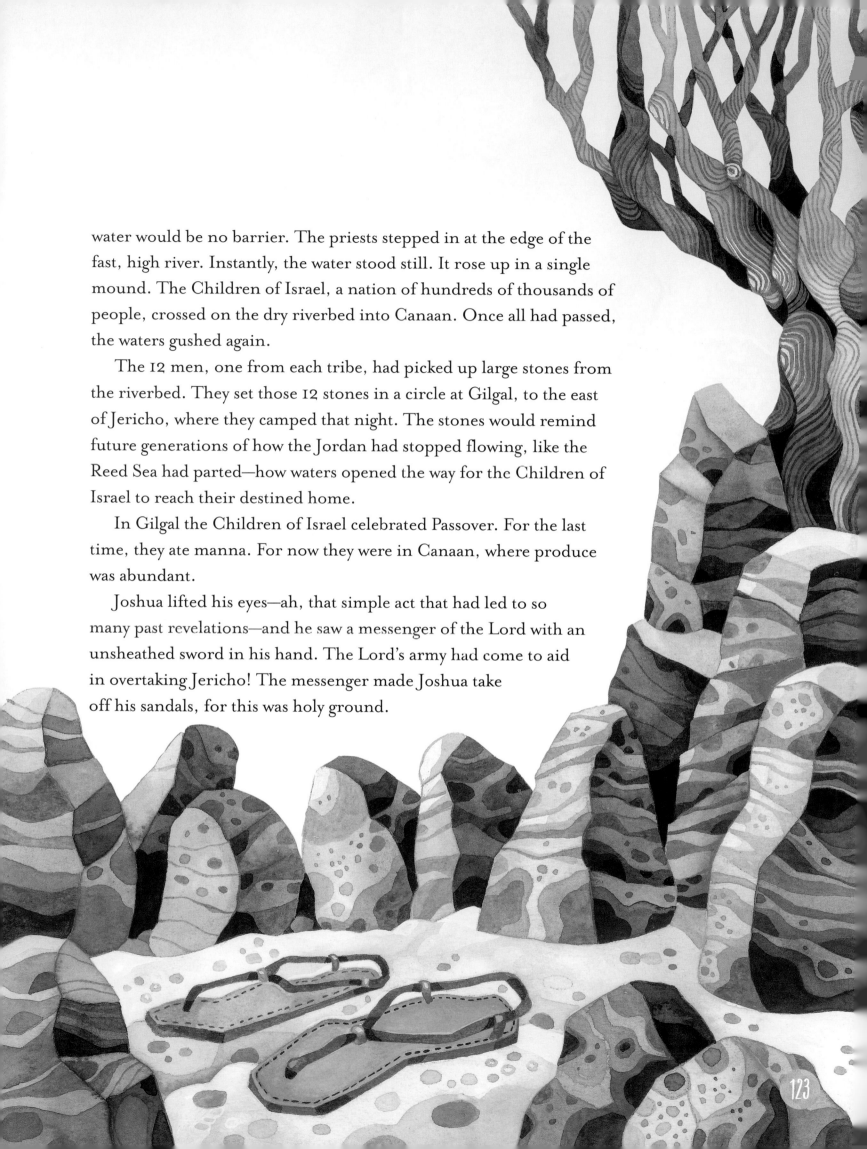

water would be no barrier. The priests stepped in at the edge of the fast, high river. Instantly, the water stood still. It rose up in a single mound. The Children of Israel, a nation of hundreds of thousands of people, crossed on the dry riverbed into Canaan. Once all had passed, the waters gushed again.

The 12 men, one from each tribe, had picked up large stones from the riverbed. They set those 12 stones in a circle at Gilgal, to the east of Jericho, where they camped that night. The stones would remind future generations of how the Jordan had stopped flowing, like the Reed Sea had parted—how waters opened the way for the Children of Israel to reach their destined home.

In Gilgal the Children of Israel celebrated Passover. For the last time, they ate manna. For now they were in Canaan, where produce was abundant.

Joshua lifted his eyes—ah, that simple act that had led to so many past revelations—and he saw a messenger of the Lord with an unsheathed sword in his hand. The Lord's army had come to aid in overtaking Jericho! The messenger made Joshua take off his sandals, for this was holy ground.

The Lord gave Joshua directions. Men carried the Ark of the Covenant once around the walls of the city of Jericho for six days. Seven priests accompanied them, blowing on ram horns. On the seventh day, they circled Jericho seven times. Then Joshua told the people, "Shout! For the Lord has given this town to us." He reminded them not to harm Rahab's clan.

The Children of Israel shouted.

The walls of Jericho came crumbling down.

The Children of Israel marched in and slaughtered men, women, children, oxen, sheep, donkeys. They burned everything but the gold, silver, bronze, and iron—which they took as treasury for the Lord's house.

All those people died.

All those animals died.

The air stank of pain.

All existence must have shrieked.

But Jericho belonged to the Children of Israel. At last.

The Children of Israel continued taking over city after city. It wasn't easy, especially since they often did evil in the eyes of the Lord and, so, suffered from the Lord's wrath. But then, battles aren't meant to be easy.

The Children of Israel surrounded Jericho, circling the walls for days, blowing on ram horns. On the seventh day, they shouted, and the walls of Jericho crumbled.

THE SITE OF JERICHO
The capture of Jericho is not based on actual history; Joshua's time would have been the late 13th century B.C.E. By then, Jericho, a former bustling metropolis, was abandoned, perhaps with no walls. But it's clear from the excavated remains that the ancient Jericho had once had thick walls and tall towers, all of which would have taken many people a long time to build. This is evidence of a structured society. It had extensive underground burial chambers and elaborate agricultural practices. On the same site another town was built around the ninth century B.C.E. and it grew big, only to be destroyed again by the Babylonians in the sixth century B.C.E. It grew once more and became the private estate of Alexander the Great in the fourth century B.C.E.

SAMSON AND DELILAH

As punishment for evil deeds, for 40 years the Lord put the Children of Israel under the power of the Philistines, from along the eastern coast of the Mediterranean Sea. During this time, among the Children of Israel lived a man named Manoah with his wife, but without children. One day a man appeared to the woman and told her not to drink wine and to eat only clean food, for she was going to have a son. No razor should touch that boy's head. He would be a servant of God—a Nazarite—who drinks no wine, eats nothing unclean, and grows his hair.

The woman told Manoah. He rushed to offer this man a meal as thanks. The man told him to make a sacrifice to God, instead. When Manoah sacrificed a kid goat, the messenger went up in the altar flames. Manoah was afraid, but the woman wasn't; this was God's wish.

When the woman gave birth, they named the babe Samson. Samson grew into a man driven by compulsions. One day he saw a beautiful Philistine woman and his heart pumped hard. He told his parents to arrange a wedding. His parents pleaded with him to choose a wife among the Children of Israel. But Samson was smitten.

On the way to visit her, Samson passed through a vineyard. A lion charged him. The spirit of the Lord seized Samson; he ripped that lion apart with his hands. He was astonished at his own strength. He told no one of this feat—perhaps he hardly believed it. He simply continued to the town where the Philistine woman lived.

After a while he visited again, this time to marry her. He stopped in the vineyard to look at the lion's remains. Yes, there it was; he had truly killed a lion. And what was this? Bees buzzed; honey pooled among the bones. Samson scooped up the glistening honey and licked it from his palms—he ate that unclean food and took some home to feed his parents.

Soon his father Manoah arranged the wedding. Samson invited 30

Previous: Samson passed through a vineyard, where a lion attacked him. To his astonishment, he killed it with his bare hands. He hadn't known his own strength before that.

companions. Impressed with his own feat, he set them this riddle:

> *From the eater came what could be eaten.*
>
> *From the fierce came what was sweet.*

If they could solve it within the seven-day wedding feast, he'd give them 30 fine cloths and 30 new garments. If they couldn't solve it, they'd have to give him the same. He was risking 30 times what each of them was risking. Still, it was unfair odds; nothing in that riddle gave a clue about the lion or honey.

They couldn't figure it out, naturally. On the fourth day, those companions took a new and vicious strategy: They threatened Samson's wife. "Lure Samson into telling you the solution, or we'll burn your and your father's home." In terror, Samson's wife badgered him, until, on the seventh day, he explained. She told the men and they then told Samson the eater was a lion and the sweet was honey.

In rage at his wife's disloyalty, Samson slew 30 Philistine men. He stole their armor and gave their garments to the riddle-solvers. Then he went home to his father's house.

After a while, Samson wanted his wife again. That's how wild his feelings were for her. But his father-in-law refused to let him in. He had thought the marriage was broken off, given how Samson's wife had betrayed him. So he'd married her to another man.

Samson shouted that he was not guilty for what he was about to do. He caught 300 foxes and tied them in pairs, tail to tail, and put a flaming torch between those tails. He set them loose among the grain, the vineyards, the olive groves. The harvest burned.

The Philistines went berserk. They burned up Samson's wife and her father, since they had caused this. But Samson could rage more than anyone. He gave those Philistines a savage thrashing, killing many, then hid in a cave near the Children of Israel.

The Philistines pursued him. The poor Children of Israel were so frightened, they told Samson they had to turn him over to the Philistines. Once they agreed not to harm Samson, he let the Philistines bind him. They brought him back to their people. The instant Samson saw his enemies, he erupted in a rage even more furious than before. He burst free, picked up the jawbone of a dead donkey, and ran through the crowds, striking at random. He killed a thousand men.

For the next 20 years, Samson led the Children of Israel.

But the Philistines were biding their time. They plotted to bring Samson down. Then Samson fell in love with another Philistine woman. Her name was Delilah, and the Philistine leaders each offered her 1,100 silver shekels if she'd find out his weak spot.

Delilah wasn't clever. She simply asked Samson how someone could bind and torture him. Samson himself may not have been clever. But in this instance he showed caution. He said, "If I were bound with seven moist leather straps, I'd become weak." The leaders gave Delilah seven wet straps. She bound him in his sleep, then announced, "The Philistines are upon you, Samson!" as the leaders exploded into the room. Samson burst those straps with a single flex of his muscles.

She tried again. Samson told her that new rope could bind and weaken him. The leaders gave Delilah new ropes. She bound Samson in his sleep, then announced, "The Philistines are upon you, Samson!" He burst those ropes like thread.

A third time she tried. Samson told her if she wove his seven braids into a web and hammered them to the wall with a peg, he'd weaken. She did. "The Philistines are upon you, Samson!" He freed himself in a snap.

Delilah badgered Samson, like his ill-fated wife had done before. And, like before, Samson caved. He had loved only two women in his

life, both in that all-encompassing way. How could he not reveal his secret to Delilah? He told her that if she cut off his hair, the hair that marked him as a Nazarite, he'd go weak. Delilah knew love made him speak truth. She laid Samson's sleeping head in her lap and shaved off his seven braids. Then she tortured the man, this woman who knew his heart and soul. "The Philistines are upon you, Samson!"

Samson woke, confused. The waiting Philistines gouged out his eyes. They imprisoned him to work grinding grain. They celebrated and had Samson brought up from prison to amuse them with his blind stumbling. They set him between the two pillars of the temple. Three thousand men and women jeered at him.

Samson asked the lad who was leading him to let him feel the pillars, that he might rest against them. He prayed. "Lord, grant me one last moment of strength." He pushed those two pillars apart. The temple crumbled, killing all within, including Samson.

The Children of Israel buried him in the grave of his father Manoah. Twenty years he'd been a leader. Stronger than anyone else. Yet love had undone him.

With a shaven head, weakened Samson prayed to the Lord for a burst of strength, then he pushed apart the pillars at his sides, making the temple fall and kill the Philistines within.

DAVID AND GOLIATH

The Children of Israel had never had a human king. There were judges, priests, and prophets as leaders. But mainly, everyone followed the Commandments and laws of the covenant, thus the Lord was their one and only ruler.

The prophet Samuel, however, was more of a leader than others. As he aged, it became clear that his sons didn't have what it took to step into his place after his death. And, oh, the people wanted a king.

Along came Saul. Tall Saul. He stood head and shoulders above the rest. If anyone looked the part of a king, Saul did. God told Samuel to give the people a king—that very Saul. So the prophet Samuel took out a horn of oil and anointed Saul king.

Then the troubles of the Children of Israel worsened. Ammonites, living to the east of the River Jordan, threatened. So did the Philistines. Moabites from the mountains, Edomites from the northwest, Zobahites from the northeast, all brought troubles, too. The Children of Israel sharpened their plowshares, axes, sickles, and mattocks, and followed Saul into raging battles. They won.

The Lord wanted Saul to annihilate the Amalekites, a long-standing enemy of the Children of Israel, down to every last beast of the field. But Saul, once he had conquered the Amalekites, stopped; he allowed some to live, especially the beasts. It seemed a waste not to take the spoils of the dead; at the least, they could be sacrificial offerings to God. This disobedience cost him his kingship: The Lord told Samuel to anoint another king—a son of the man Jesse in Bethlehem.

What? Saul was king. And he led a formidable army. Samuel feared that if Saul heard of a second king, he would kill him. In secret, Samuel went to Jesse's home, where Jesse paraded his seven sons in front of him. But the Lord didn't choose any of them.

"Don't you have any other boy?" asked Samuel.

Previous: David was but a slight boy, the youngest of his brothers, who tended sheep and had a mild manner. He hardly looked like the king he was about to become.

"I do. The youngest." Jesse shrugged. "He's tending sheep."

Samuel nodded. That must be who the Lord wanted. "Fetch him."

This last son, David, was a ruddy boy, handsome with bright eyes. David was not kingly to look at—his father hadn't considered him worthy of mention. But Samuel understood that the Lord had had enough of kingly appearances; it was time for a king chosen by the heart, not the eyes. Someone obedient, who paid attention, like Moses. Samuel poured oil from his horn a second time, and anointed David as king of the Children of Israel.

Still Saul knew nothing of this. But an evil spirit entered him; he was afraid all the time. His servants said he needed a good lyre player to soothe him. They chose none other than David, the son of Jesse, the secret second king. Whenever Saul's nerves made him miserable, David played. Saul felt relief and came to love the boy. Saul was so kind; David's own father had never been that kind.

Meanwhile the Philistines gathered for another attack. Among them was a tall, strong man named Goliath, dressed in armor, with a bronze helmet and a spear that weighed 600 iron shekels. Goliath challenged the Children of Israel to produce someone to fight him, man-to-man, and thus avoid a war. The people of the loser would be slaves to the people of the winner. At that time, David was near the Philistines, for his father Jesse had sent him to bring provisions to his older brothers in Saul's army. Why would David's father do that, given the stature of that boy? Was he like Joseph's father Jacob-Israel, who sent him out to his brothers knowing full well how they despised him? But David was

The boy David was sure the Lord would rescue him as he fought the big man Goliath. He had only a slingshot and stones, while Goliath had a huge sword. But David was right; it was he who won.

happy to go. He was fascinated by Goliath's challenge. When his brothers realized this, they scorned him. All the same, David offered to fight Goliath for the Children of Israel.

"You're just a boy," said Saul. "He's a warrior."

"I've fought off lion and bear when they've come to threaten my father's flock. The Lord who rescued me from them will rescue me from this Philistine."

Saul put his armor on David, but it was so big, slight David couldn't walk in it. Instead, David went in his ordinary clothes, a stick in one hand, five smooth stones from the creek in his pouch, and a slingshot in the other hand. Goliath was offended when he saw this puny fellow. "I'll feed your flesh to birds and beasts." David invoked God and made his own threats. Then he took out his slingshot. The very first stone struck Goliath in the forehead. He fell flat on his face. David grabbed Goliath's sword, massive though it was, and slew him. The Philistines fled.

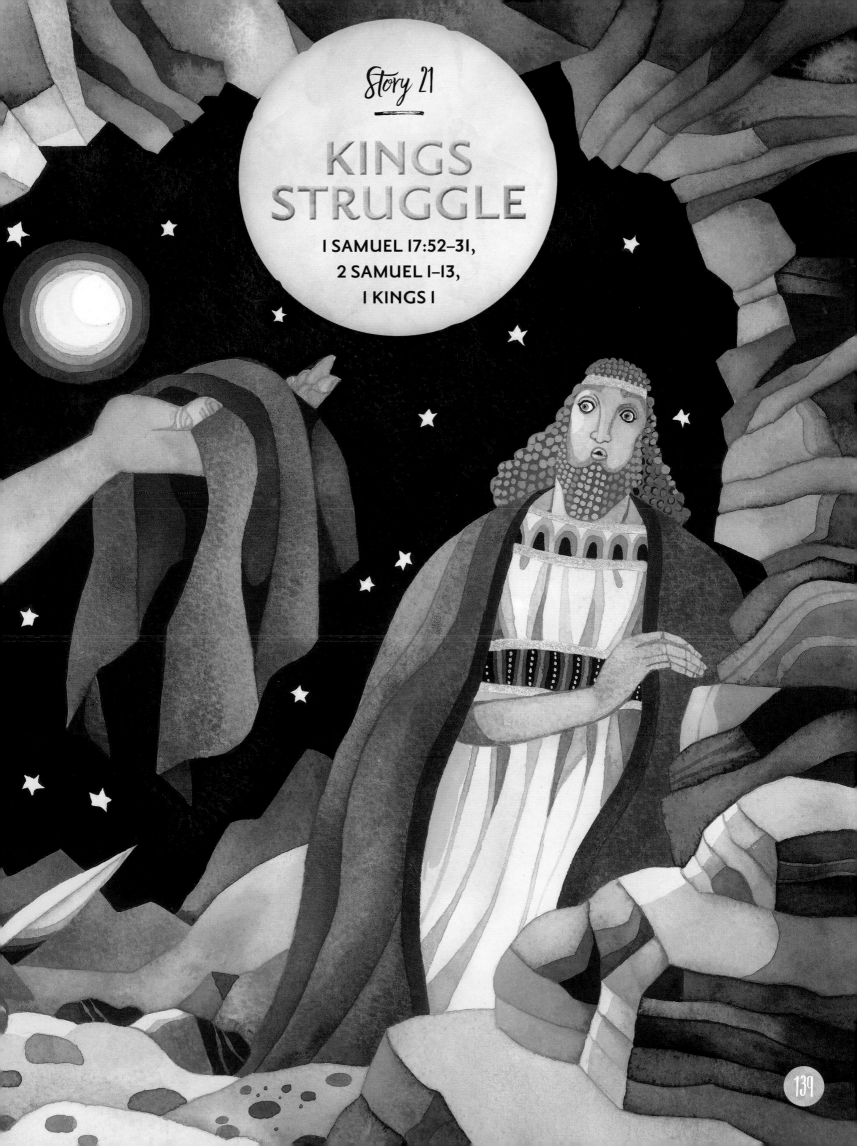

Story 21

KINGS STRUGGLE

1 SAMUEL 17:52–31,
2 SAMUEL 1–13,
1 KINGS 1

KINGS STRUGGLE

After defeating Goliath, David returned to Saul's home. Saul was amazed to realize the victor was his lyre boy. Women danced in the streets with timbrels and lutes, singing,

Saul killed thousands, and David, tens of thousands.

The words grated on Saul. But Saul's son Jonathan loved David more than a true brother. Jonathan gave David his cloak and battle gear, and they fit perfectly. It was as though their souls joined, as though Jonathan was ceding to David what was his as heir to Saul, even the kingship. David wore Jonathan's battle gear into more wars and won. Everywhere he went, women sang,

Saul killed thousands, and David, tens of thousands.

Saul grew ever more suspicious of David. One day he threw his spear at the boy … twice. But David was quick. So Saul sent David to wage more wars. He promised his older daughter to him … then changed his mind and gave her to another. He promised his younger daughter, Michal, to him. This time they wed, and David was happy.

But Saul's fears grew. The Lord was with David, not with Saul. No one could beat David in a war. Everyone loved him. The women sang,

Saul killed thousands, and David, tens of thousands.

Saul lost his mind to jealousy and self-doubt. He tried to kill David, chasing him into the wilderness. He put to death those he thought conspired in favor of David. It must have been excruciating for David, given how he revered Saul. But Saul's son Jonathan saved David repeatedly, as did Saul's daughter Michal. They realized God had chosen him to be king of the Children of Israel. Every time Saul sent David into battle, no matter how bad the odds, he survived.

Once Saul entered a cave to relieve himself, not knowing that David and his soldiers were deep inside. The soldiers urged David to kill Saul. David snuck up behind Saul and cut off a bit of his cloak. When

Previous: David snuck up behind Saul in a cave and cut off a part of his cloak. Then he showed him, so that Saul would know David could have killed him but never would. He loved Saul like a boy loves his father.

Another time David stole Saul's water jug and spear while he slept. He could have killed him that time, too, but he refused to. He still loved Saul.

Saul exited the cave, David followed and knelt before him.

"Father, see this bit of cloak. My men said I should kill you, but I would never do that. You are my king, anointed by God." David had called Saul "father." His heart was breaking.

"Is that the voice of my son David?" answered Saul, barely able to believe his eyes. His agony equaled David's, and his words echoed those of the bedridden Isaac when Jacob-Israel had entered disguised as Esau. All Saul could do was weep; he'd been wrong. "You will be king," he said, though perhaps he realized that David was already king. "Swear you'll never wipe out my descendants." So those terrible fears persisted, even in this moment of proof of David's loyalty.

David swore.

Around this time the prophet Samuel died. The Children of Israel mourned, especially David. The cold fact now settled inside David: Samuel's anointing him had lasting effects. Saul would always want David dead. David had to stay wary. This fact made him more responsive to kindness from others. A wicked man refused to give provisions to David's troops. But his wife Abigail loaded donkeys with bread, wine, sheep, grain, raisin cakes, fig cakes, and brought them to David, for she admired this man of the Children of Israel. The husband was so upset at this betrayal that he died. David rewarded Abigail by making her his second wife. Then he took a third wife, Ahinoam. But Saul cut through any pleasure David might have had, for Saul broke the law and gave his own daughter Michal, David's first wife, to another man.

Saul led 3,000 skilled troops after David, whose soldiers were a motley group of a few hundred disenfranchised men. While Saul lay asleep in the wilderness with his troops, David came across him. Again, David's men urged him to slay his enemy. David stole Saul's spear and water jug. He went to high ground and called out, saying the troops needed to do a better job protecting Saul, for, lo, he had easily taken Saul's spear and water jug, the two tools crucial for survival.

Saul woke. "Is that the voice of my son David?"

Hearing himself called "son" again must have pierced David's heart. "It is, my king."

David returned the spear and Saul admitted wrongdoing. But things had changed. David was a bloodthirsty warrior now. He wiped out towns, leaving no one alive, taking sheep, cattle, donkeys, camels—raiding the households of the dead. As for Saul, he was a beaten man. Soon Saul's sons, including Jonathan, were killed in a battle with the Philistines. Saul threw himself on his sword to avoid capture.

When David learned of their deaths, he sang a song of sorrow … the first of many songs that would flow from his heart … for he had lost a father, no matter how fickle, and a brother as true as purity.

Then he publicly owned his kingship. But warring continued. The northern lands were still fighting—as though in memory of dead Saul—against the southern lands, who embraced David. That northern branch were descendants of Joseph and of Benjamin, the sons of Jacob-Israel with his wife Rachel. That southern branch were descendants of Judah, the son of Jacob-Israel with his wife Leah. Though the family had reconciled, that reconciliation was not firm, for the cleft remained apparent still. The Lord helped David win the war, until all Children of Israel united under their king, completing the reconciliation.

A part of David was nourished by the boy within who had played the lyre to soothe the souls of others and by the man within who sang the lamentation psalm at Saul's and Jonathan's deaths. This part of David lifted up Mephibosheth, the son of Jonathan, lame in both feet, and gave him Saul's belongings and brought him to eat at his table. Thus David protected the vulnerable.

Another part of David was nourished by the boy within who had challenged the towering Goliath, and by the man within who had waged battle and won. This part took wife after wife: Maacah, Haggith, Abital, Eglah. This part looked through David's eyes one hot night as he stood on his roof and saw a beautiful woman bathing. Her name was Bathsheba. Her husband, the Hittite Uriah, was off in battle. David had Bathsheba brought to him, and he loved her. When she became pregnant with his child, he had Uriah sent into the thickest part of battle; Uriah died there. David married Bathsheba and she bore him a son. Thus David exploited the vulnerable.

The Lord sent the prophet Nathan to tell David a story about two men, one rich, one poor. The rich man had many sheep and cattle. The poor man had but one lamb, who ate from his cup and slept in his lap. A traveler came to the rich man's house. Instead of making a meal from one of his own sheep, he made a meal of the poor man's lamb.

David raged. "The rich man was wrong! He should pay back the poor man four times over!"

"You are the rich man," said Nathan. Uriah was the poor man. David would have to pay four times over for his sin.

The son Bathsheba bore to David fell ill. For seven days, David fasted and prayed, but the boy died. That was payment number one. David's oldest son Amnon was cruel to his half-sister Tamar. Payment number two. Absalom, Tamar's full brother, killed Amnon in retaliation. Payment number three. Absalom mounted a rebellion against David and was killed. Payment number four.

David's story played itself out to an ever sadder tune. Famine, battles, intrigues. But one good thing happened: Bathsheba gave David another son. David called him Solomon, while the prophet Nathan called him Jedidiah. David knew this boy would improve life for the Children of Israel. When King David lay dying, he declared Solomon heir to the throne.

BATTLE GEAR
In this tale, Jonathan gives David his cloak and, even more important, his battle gear: armor, sword, bow, and belt, just as his father Saul had tried to do when David first came to him as a boy, far too small to wear the king's armor. Giving apparel and weapons has strong significance in the ancient world in general. In the Greek epic *The Iliad*, two warriors who were supposed to be on opposite sides, Glaucus and Diomedes, learn that their grandfathers had been friends; to show respect for this old friendship, they exchange armor. That way, they are essentially protecting the other with the same means and vehemence that they would use to protect themselves.

SOLOMON'S WISDOM

1 KINGS 2–11

SOLOMON'S WISDOM

King David's great accomplishment was to unite the Children of Israel. King Solomon's great accomplishment was to maintain that unity. For 40 years he would reign over an unshakable people. The Lord had promised David and then Solomon that, so long as the Commandments and laws were followed, the Lord would support and protect the Children of Israel. But Solomon was more than a unifier; he was wise.

Solomon went to the town of Gibeon and prepared a sacrifice to the Lord, in the form of 1,000 burnt offerings. That night God came in his dream. "Ask!" God said. "What shall I give you?"

Solomon said God had been kind to his father David and God had been kind to Solomon himself. But Solomon was young and inexperienced, so he was cowed by how many people he had to rule, especially since those people had repeatedly proved themselves unruly. He asked for an understanding heart. That way he could tell what was good from what was not and have a chance at ruling decently.

What a fine request! Solomon had not been greedy; he had not asked for long life or wealth or the death of his enemies. He had put the people first. God granted a wisdom never before given and never to be given again, a wisdom that Solomon had, in fact, already demonstrated by virtue of his request. Because of Solomon's selflessness, God also promised him long life and wealth.

When Solomon returned to Jerusalem, two women of ill repute came to him to resolve their argument.

"We live in the same house. I gave birth to a son. Three days later she did the same. Her baby smothered in the night because she rolled over on him. She put her dead babe beside me as I slept and took my live babe as hers. When I woke, I saw that the dead child beside me was not mine."

Previous: Two women claimed a baby as their own. Who knew which told the truth? So King Solomon ordered the child to be cut in half—half for each woman. One woman begged him not to and to instead give the child to the other woman. Wise King Solomon gave the child to the begging woman.

"Liar. My son is the living one; yours is the dead one."

"No! Just the reverse."

They continued like that until King Solomon said, "Fetch my sword." The servant brought the sword. "Cut the child in two. Each woman will get half."

"Stop! I beseech you, give the boy to her. Do not put him to death."

"Go ahead! Cut him in half. Neither of us shall have a son."

King Solomon nodded. "Give the living boy to the woman who would keep him alive. She is his mother."

Perhaps she was his mother, perhaps not. Either way, the one who would have the child live was the right one to raise him. Solomon's wisdom put all Israel in awe; this king knew about justice. This king knew how to lead. His father David had suffered as a leader because he wanted Saul to love him. But Solomon moved with the confidence of having God's love. He showed it not just in his judgments, but in the fact that he wrote 3,000 proverbs and 5,000 poems about wisdom, justice, love, and righteousness. His understanding was vast as the grains of sand on the seashore—vast as the offspring God had promised Abraham years before. King Solomon was a botanist, talking about everything from the simple wall moss to the great cedars of Lebanon. He was a biologist, talking about beasts, birds, creeping things, and fish. People from everywhere came to learn about life on earth from Solomon. Kings sent representatives to learn from him. Solomon built a palace for the Lord. Colossal, with fine windows and a balcony around the great hall, paneled in cedar, overlaid with gold—this sanctuary took a full seven years to build. The Lord promised to dwell in it, like the Lord had promised to dwell in the tabernacle Moses built. Solomon spread his palms to the heavens and talked on and on about the glory of God, about how heavens could not contain God, so how

King Solomon loved wealth far too much. Even the wealthy Queen of Sheba was in awe of the splendor of his home. They exchanged precious gifts.

could this house Solomon had built ever do that. He begged the Lord to be with them, sustain them through offenses when they sought forgiveness, give them rain, and aid in times of famine, plague, blight, mildew, locusts, caterpillars, enemy attacks. Whatever afflicted the heart, the Lord should be merciful and give balm. Solomon knew that the most important thing was for the people to have a strong relationship with God. God promised to do these things, so long as the people obeyed the Commandments and laws.

Still, Solomon had flaws. While he had not shown greed to God in that earlier dream, he now displayed outrageous greed, though Moses had long ago warned against a king having too much wealth. King Solomon charged his subjects for securing the peace: flour, oxen, sheep, deer, gazelle, roebuck, fatted geese. He had 40,000 stalls for his 1,400 chariots and 12,000 horsemen, and silver as plentiful as stones of the field. He spent 13 years building his house, decorated with bronze pomegranates and birds flying around a cast-metal sea. When the Queen of Sheba came from Ethiopia to test Solomon's wisdom with riddles, she was breathless as much at this splendor as at his answers. She gave him gold and spices. He gave her sandalwood and precious stones.

But the most dangerous thing Solomon did involved women. Moses had warned that too many wives would lead a king's heart astray. This rich king took 700 wives and loved even more women, some Children of Israel and some not, though the Lord had forbidden marriage with foreigners for fear the wives would then turn their husbands away from the one true God. That's exactly what happened to Solomon. For love of his wives, he adhered to the goddess Ashtoreth of the Sidonians, to the gods Milcom and Molech of the Ammonites, and to the god Chemosh of the Moabites. The Lord was furious. Out of respect for David, who had united the people, King Solomon would be allowed to rule till his death. But when the throne passed to his son Rehoboam, the Lord would tear away the kingdom and give it to another. To Rehoboam the Lord would leave only one tribe.

BIBLICAL KING SOLOMON
Biblical characters often employed the same practices to gain and maintain control as historical figures have done in times since, perhaps giving us evidence of what was considered a sensible path to power in ancient times. In the First Book of Kings, we learn three important things about Solomon: He was wise, so he knew how to judge fairly and write proverbs and songs. He was a renowned botanist and biologist, and people traveled from all over to learn from him. Finally, he had many wives, and this was his worst flaw. While that might have been his worst flaw spiritually, in fact, through strategic and multiple marriages, King Solomon made alliances across Africa, India, and the Arabian Peninsula, allowing him to control many trade routes and to keep the Children of Israel safe and prosperous.

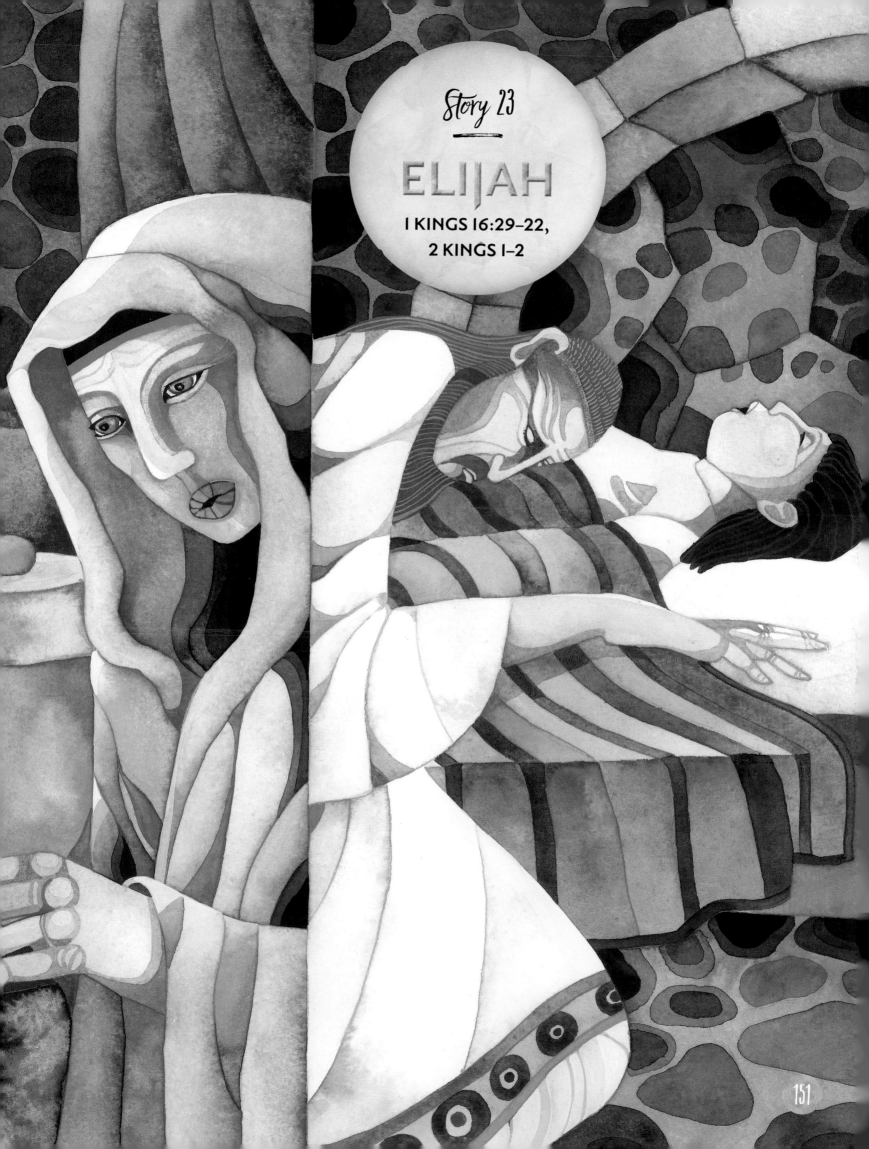

ELIJAH

Many years later, during the reign of King Ahab, things did not go well for the Children of Israel. Ahab married a foreign woman named Jezebel, who worshipped the god Baal and led Ahab to do the same. Upon her orders, prophets of the Lord were killed.

The Lord was irate. Why did these Children of Israel keep making the same annoying mistake, worshipping false gods?

So the only remaining prophet of the Lord, Elijah—a hairy man who wore a leather belt—told King Ahab that rain would not fall again until the Lord decided it would. This was amazing. How could this hairy Elijah's god control the weather? Ahab didn't believe him.

Elijah went to a wadi—a riverbed—and drank. Ravens came every sunrise and sunset and fed Elijah bread and meat. This was Elijah's first miracle.

After a while a drought came and the wadi dried up. The Lord told Elijah to go to a town where a widow would sustain him. Elijah went to the town of Zarephath and saw a widow gathering sticks. He asked for water, which she gave. But when he asked for bread, she said she had but a handful of flour and only drops of oil. She would use them to make bread for her son and herself, and still they would die. Elijah assured her that if she fed him, the flour jar would not go empty nor would the oil cruse go empty, not until it rained again. So the widow fed Elijah, and sure enough, there was still flour and oil left. This was Elijah's second miracle.

After many days the widow's son got sick and died. She railed at Elijah: "You came and killed my son." Elijah bade her bring him her son. He carried the body upstairs to his chamber and lay him on the bed. He stretched himself over the boy's body three times and begged the Lord to bring back life-breath. Suddenly the boy breathed again. This was Elijah's third miracle. "See?" he said to the widow. The

Previous: The prophet Elijah went to a riverbed with no food; ravens came and fed him bread and meat. Next Elijah went to a widow's house and promised her that if she fed him, her flour and oil would not run out; it was true. Finally, when the widow's son died, Elijah lay upon him and he came back to life. These were Elijah's three miracles.

widow knew then that Elijah was a true man of God.

The drought dragged on for three more years. Finally Elijah and Ahab had a showdown. Ahab said, "Is that you, you troubler of Israel?"

"It's you who made the trouble. Bring everyone to me," said Elijah. "The Children of Israel and the prophets of Baal and Asherah—these men who eat at your wife Jezebel's table. It's time for a gathering at Mount Carmel."

When a crowd had assembled, Elijah addressed them. "Why do you hop from one god to another? If you believe in the Lord, God of Israel, follow that one. If you believe in Baal, follow that one."

No one spoke.

"All right then, a challenge. I am the only remaining prophet of the Lord. But there are 450 prophets of Baal. Let the prophets of Baal slaughter a bull for sacrifice and put it on the altar, but not light the fire. I will do the same. We can pray to our gods for fire to consume the sacrifice. The god who answers first is the true God."

The prophets of Baal prepared a bull. They jumped around on the altar, calling to Baal. They called all morning. At noon, Elijah mocked them, saying perhaps they should call louder, for maybe Baal was asleep or traveling. The prophets of Baal called louder and cut themselves with their own swords and seemed to lose their minds.

Elijah repaired the altar—for it had been damaged by the jumping. He took 12 stones, one for each of the tribes of Israel, and made the altar strong. He cut up his bull and lay it on the bed of sticks. He dug a trench around the altar and told the people to pour four jugs of water over the offering and the firewood. He made them do that three times, until everything was soaked and the trench was full to the brim. By this time, it was the hour of the afternoon offering. Elijah called to the Lord, God of Israel. Just like that, fire consumed the offering and

licked up the water till the trench was dry.

The people fell on their faces in worship of the Lord. Elijah told them to kill the prophets of Baal. Wretched act. Perhaps being the lone remaining prophet of the Lord had cost him whatever mercy he might have had.

Elijah climbed Mount Carmel and looked out over the Mediterranean Sea. He told the men who followed him to look, too. They saw nothing. Seven times he told them to look, until finally they saw a small cloud, like a man's palm rising from the waters. "Go tell Ahab to hurry home before the rain hits and the road is too muddy for travel."

Ahab went home. Elijah went the opposite direction, for he knew that Jezebel would order him killed. No one would defend him; no one truly had faith. He felt ready to die; the struggle had gone on too long. He fell asleep and woke to a meal of bread and water, brought by an angel. For 40 days and nights he wandered, eating only what the angel brought. Then he stopped in a cave. The Lord said, "Why are you here?"

"I am moved by zeal for the Lord. But the Children of Israel have made a mess. I alone remain faithful … and they want to kill me."

"Stand on the mountain and look as the Lord passes."

A great wind tore apart the mountain, but the Lord was not in that wind. An earthquake shook, but the Lord was not in that earthquake. Fire raged, but the Lord was not in that fire. Then came the sound of thin quiet, like a still, small voice.

Elijah wrapped his mantel around his face and stood at the mouth of the cave.

"Why are you here? Go home, Elijah."

ELIJAH, THE VISITOR
Passover begins with a Seder, a special dinner. After the meal, people open their house door to invite the prophet Elijah to enter and confirm that they are ready for him. People fill five cups with wine, but reserve one for Elijah, who they believe will visit right before the redemption day. Elijah is said to bring world peace and clear up confusion people have about religion. This prophet is one of the most beloved figures of the western religions of Judaism, Catholicism, and Islam.

Elijah challenged the prophets of Baal to see whose god could make a fire under a sacrificed bull faster. The firewood of those who believed in Baal never set flame, but Elijah's set flame the first time he called to the Lord. All this was done to convince the people who was the true god.

Elijah went back home.

While all this was going on, Ahab got a yearning for the vineyard of his neighbor Naboth, but Naboth would not sell it. Ahab sulked. He wouldn't eat. Jezebel promised she'd get that vineyard for him. She wrote letters in Ahab's name, sealed them with Ahab's seal, and sent them to the elders. The letters denounced Naboth for cursing god and king, and gave the names of two men—scoundrels—who would bear witness to that—false witness, of course. So Naboth was stoned to death. Ahab got his vineyard for free.

The moment reeked of treachery as evil as what David had done to Bathsheba's husband. The Lord told Elijah to confront Ahab and tell him that the very place in which dogs lapped up Naboth's blood would be the place that dogs would lap up Ahab's blood.

When Ahab heard this, he wailed, rending his clothes. Then he wore sackcloth, fasted, and wandered around, humbled by the evil he and his wife had done. The Lord had mercy on Ahab, but not on his children. Thus the father didn't experience disaster, but the children did.

Later, after Ahab died, God announced that Elisha would succeed Elijah as prophet. When it was time for Elijah to go to the heavens, Elisha begged Elijah to give him double his spirit, for he feared that he wasn't up to taking over for Elijah. Then a chariot of fire separated the two, and Elijah disappeared in a whirlwind. Elisha picked up Elijah's mantle, which had fallen, rolled it up, and struck the water of the River Jordan. The water parted—like it had parted for Joshua.

From then on, if people wanted to know what the Lord was thinking, they turned to the spirit of the prophet Elijah. They called him the elusive one, the wanderer, the one who maybe never died. They thought he might be the harbinger of the Messiah, when the world is finally ready for perfection.

Story 24

JONAH AND THE GIANT FISH

BOOK OF JONAH

JONAH AND THE GIANT FISH

Jonah was an ordinary man, living his ordinary life, when the Lord said, "Get up! Go to the great city of Nineveh and call out to the people, telling them the right way to live, because their wickedness has come to my attention."

This was not good news. Nineveh was the capital of the Assyrian empire. It was a place where the many poor suffered badly as the few rich indulged themselves. Violence ruled the streets. Who could be persuasive enough to correct such corruption? Like Moses before him, Jonah had never asked for such responsibility. He felt sure this would not turn out well for him. But unlike Moses, Jonah did not try to talk the Lord into choosing someone else. He fled.

Jonah went to the town of Joppa, on the shore of the Mediterranean Sea, and boarded a ship headed for the city of Tarshish. He thought he could sneak away without the Lord knowing. The Lord knew, of course. The Lord sent a mighty wind, for wind had been a fine divine tool since Day One of the creation. The ship was buffeted about so hard, it threatened to fall apart. The sailors were not members of the tribes of Israel, so they prayed to their various gods for salvation, as they threw cargo overboard to lighten the ship and make it easier to steer. Meanwhile Jonah lay below deck, asleep. The captain woke him. "Get up! Call out to your god for salvation!"

Jonah went to the deck, where the sailors had decided to cast lots to figure out whose fault it was that they were in such peril. The lot pointed to Jonah!

"What did you do?" They wanted to know all about him.

"I'm a Hebrew. I worship the Lord who made heaven, sea, earth."

"But what did you do to make our troubles now?"

"I ran from the Lord."

"How can we get the storm to stop?"

Previous: The Lord gave Jonah a task, but it was too huge, so Jonah escaped in a boat. But the Lord sent a wind that would capsize the boat if the men didn't throw Jonah overboard. Seeing no way out, the men did that, and Jonah sank through the sea into the waiting jaws of a giant fish.

"Lift me up and throw me into the sea. Abandon me. For the storm is my fault."

The men were horrified. They didn't want to murder an innocent man; they rowed ever harder for shore. But the sea grew wilder. They prayed to Jonah's god, asking that they not be given blame for Jonah's death, since that was what the Lord wanted. And they picked up Jonah and threw him overboard. Instantly, the sea calmed. The frightened men changed their loyalty in astonishment. They offered a sacrifice to the Lord.

Jonah thrashed about in the salty water. Seaweed wrapped around his head. He sank as deep as the roots of the mountains, when a giant fish swallowed him whole. He spent the next three days and nights inside that fish. What glories of the undersea world must he have seen through the glassy eyes of that monstrous fish! He prayed the whole time.

The Lord listened to Jonah's prayers and commanded the fish to spit Jonah onto dry land. But that didn't mean Jonah's ordeal was over. Oh, no, the Lord wasn't about to let up on Jonah. "Get up," the Lord ordered again. "Go to the great city of Nineveh and deliver my message."

This time Jonah went. Nineveh was so huge, it would take a person three days to walk from one end to the other. Jonah walked just one day into the city and announced, "In forty days' time, God will destroy this evil city."

The people believed Jonah. Who knows why? He was just an ordinary man walking through the streets,

THE GREAT FISH
Jonah is swallowed by a *dag gadol*—(דג גדול) "great fish." The Mediterranean has huge groupers and several kinds of sharks, including the great white. It also has two very large whales: the fin whale and the sperm whale. Whales generally don't swallow prey whole, but groupers and sharks do—though passage through the esophagus would be rough. Could a human survive if swallowed? Air supply would be cut off. Digestive juices would break down flesh and bones. So the Jonah story must be read as miracle or metaphor.

shouting. They could as easily have thought he was a lunatic. Yet they listened and feared God. They put on sackcloth to show they repented of their indulgences. Even the king repented. He shed his royal robes, put on sackcloth, and sat in ashes, as he proclaimed a fast. No people or animals should drink or eat. Everyone must give up evil and violent ways. The king hoped that God would see their repentance and turn from anger, treating them kindly.

And God did. No destruction came.

Jonah thought this was the worst thing that could happen to a prophet. Here Jonah had proclaimed coming destruction and what did God do? God turned from anger—making Jonah a false prophet. No destruction came. Jonah was furious. "I knew you'd be compassionate, Lord. That's why I didn't want to deliver your message. Kill me now. Death is better than life."

The Lord asked, "Is it right for you to be angry?"

In silence, Jonah went outside the city to the east and made a shelter. He watched to see what would become of the city. God made a kikayon plant grow tall and throw shade over Jonah, who was happy not just for the respite it offered but for its company.

The next day God sent a worm that ate the kikayon. Jonah watched, aghast. The poor plant!

God sent an east wind that scorched Jonah, and a sun that blazed his head. Faint and weary, Jonah declared again, "Kill me now. Death is better than life."

The Lord answered, "You felt mercy for the kikayon, though you did not tend it, you did not make it grow. Do you then say that I should not feel mercy for the people of Nineveh, 120,000 people, and that many animals, as well?"

What could Jonah respond? The Lord was right, of course. Thus Jonah's story ends. He was God's agent, even though it brought him no personal glory. That was the fate of prophets.

The Lord made Jonah his prophet, and had him spread the news that the city of Nineveh would be destroyed for its evil ways. But the Lord relented when the people repented. In despair, Jonah made a shelter outside the city and sat under a kikayon plant that God made grow, and lamented being a false prophet.

163

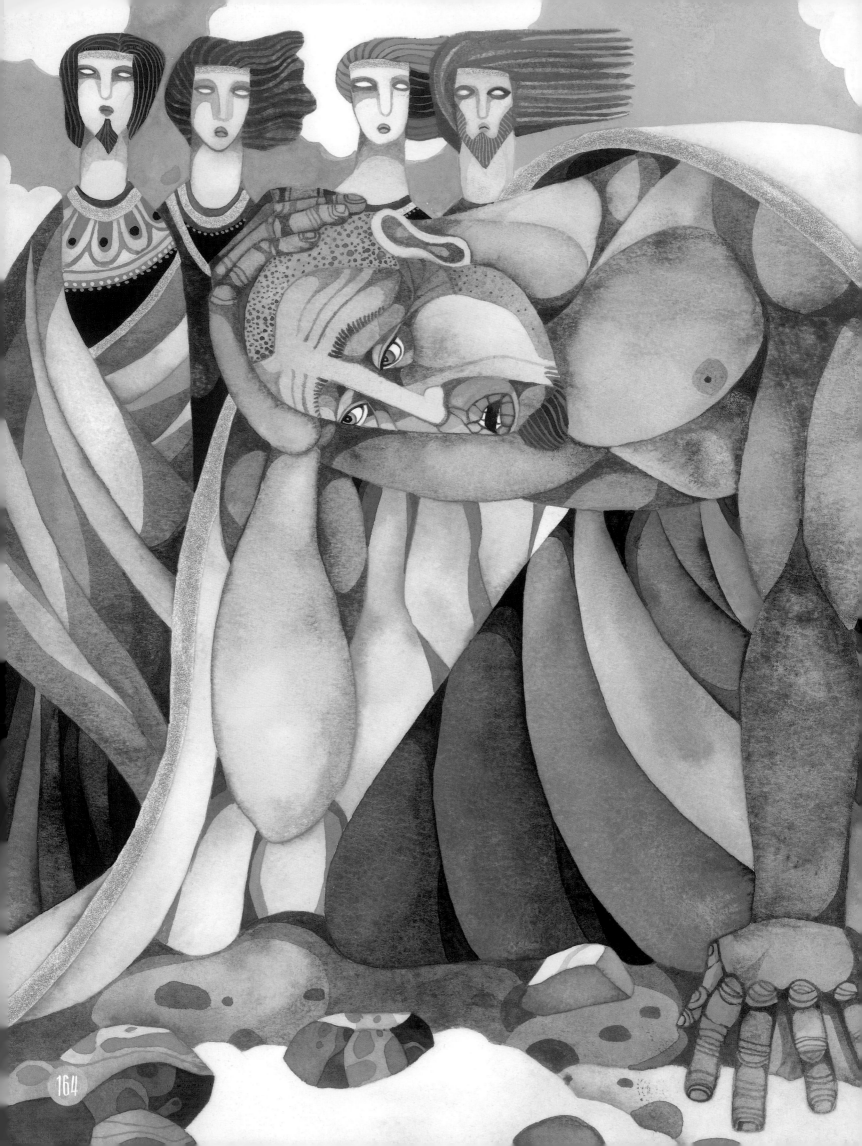

JOB'S AFFLICTIONS

Job had everything going for him. He had seven sons, three daughters, 7,000 sheep, 3,000 camels, 500 pairs of yoked oxen, 500 jenny donkeys, and a huge household. He was faithful to the Lord. He often made burnt offerings to the Lord for all his family, just in case his children had been remiss.

One day the *satan*, an adversary, came before the Lord.

"Where have you come from?" asked the Lord.

"Wandering the earth."

"Have you noticed my servant Job? He's upright and faithful."

"Of course," said the adversary. "You've blessed everything he does. But if you make problems for him, he'll curse you."

The Lord rose to the bait. "All right. Everything Job has is in your hands. Only do not harm him."

Soon after that, a messenger arrived at Job's home. "The Sabeans killed your oxen, donkeys, and the servants guarding them. I alone escaped."

While he was yet speaking, a second messenger arrived. "Fire fell from heaven and burned up your sheep and shepherds. I alone escaped."

While he was yet speaking, a third messenger arrived. "The Chaldeans stole your camels and killed the servants guarding them. I alone escaped."

While he was yet speaking, a fourth messenger arrived, with the worst news. "Your children were feasting at your oldest son's home when a wind swept across the wilderness and flattened the house. It crushed them dead. I alone escaped."

Job cried out, rending his robe. He shaved his head, fell to his knees, and prayed. "The Lord has given and the Lord has taken away. May the Lord's name be blessed."

So the Lord won that cruel bet.

Previous: Four men came to Job, each bearing horrendous news: His oxen and donkeys and their guards had died, his sheep and shepherds had died, his camels had been stolen and his servants killed, and, worst of all, his children had died. Job sank to the ground in grief and prayer.

The adversary came again to the Lord, and again the Lord asked, "Where have you come from?"

"Wandering the earth."

"Have you noticed my servant Job? You led me to destroy everything he had for no reason, yet he is faithful to me."

"Skin for skin," said the adversary. "A man can give up all he has. But if you harm his bone and flesh, he'll curse you."

Again the Lord responded. "All right. He is in your hands. Only do not kill him."

Job was struck with sores head to foot. Job sat in ashes and scraped at the burning sores with broken pottery. His wife said, "Why do you remain faithful? Curse god and die." At least that way Job would be freed of this last pain. But Job refused to speak against the Lord.

Three friends came to comfort Job: Eliphaz the Temanite, Bildad the Shuhite, and Zophar the Naamathite. For seven days and nights they sat with him. At last Job spoke: "Perish the day I was born." He wailed. "Let darkness foul that day." He wept. "Let that night be barren, with no song of joy." The worst that he had ever dreaded had befallen him. His death-wish poem made the air ache. His anguish made the ground shiver.

Eliphaz spoke first. He said innocent men never suffered. So clearly Job was not innocent. Job had sinned. He had drunk wrongdoing like water. He must look inside himself, see that sin, and repent.

Job protested. He was innocent. Job had not asked for gifts, nor had he offered bribes. He behaved with integrity always. Job demanded that someone explain to him how he had gone astray. He was not some monster from the sea. He was a good man who now loathed his life.

Bildad spoke next. No human was innocent. The very essence of being human made one a sinner. Even the moon and the stars were not bright in the eyes of God. So how could humans be bright? Humans were worms. Job deserved whatever God gave him.

Job protested again. Of course God was all powerful and of course Job could not answer God in a test of arguments. All Job wanted was a chance to speak and know why God condemned him and ask for mercy. God made Job, after all. How could God simply turn away?

Now Zophar spoke. No, Job did not see his own sins. But that didn't mean he hadn't sinned. God saw every iniquity. Job's sins were like the venom of cobras within him. God rained burning anger on the bodies of sinners.

No, protested Job. God could humble anyone—God could make chiefs grope in the dark and stagger like drunkards. Yet Job deserved a chance to argue his case with God. He would speak—that's all—then let come what may. Even a felled tree might hope to sprout again.

On and on they argued, until Job called them fickle friends. They told him to be patient as God afflicted him.

Weeping reddened Job's face; his prayer was pure. Surely God should put a stop to this and kill him now. Job would never speak against God. But he had to know: Where would wisdom be found? Job had had everything. Now he had nothing. Everyone shunned him. He was the definition of affliction. Blameless, distraught, sick of life. Many wicked prospered, but Job wasn't wicked. Job called out for a fair trial.

A fourth friend of Job arrived: Elihu the Buzite. Elihu was angry that Job dared challenge God. The truth was that God spoke in many ways. In visions that came in dreams, in pain that takes away appetite. This is God's warning, said Elihu. Job should pay attention, so that his soul could be brought back from the pit. By rebelling against God's wishes, Job added to his sins. Elihu closed his speech with the claim: God is majestic and does only right.

Finally the Lord spoke to Job. "Who is this who speaks without knowledge?" The Lord went on with question after question. "Where were you when I created the earth … the morning stars … the seashores?" "Have you commanded the morning since your days began?" "Have you entered the springs of the sea or walked in its depths?" "Have you entered the reserves of snow or hail?" "Have you carved a path through torrential rain for the thunderbolt?" "Can you hunt prey for the lion and nourish the cubs in their dens or thickets?" "Do you know the season when the mountain goats give birth?" "Who makes a donkey swift … the wild ox willing to serve you?" "Who understands the waving plumage of an ostrich wing?" "Did you give the horse its mane?" "Does your wisdom help the hawk soar?" Anyone who argued with God must answer such questions.

"I am small—a lightweight," Job said, and put his hand over his mouth, in awe at the vastness of God's powers.

The Lord came in a whirlwind and listed many things no man could do, things the Lord did. The Lord urged Job to clothe himself in the glory and mystery of God.

"I spoke without understanding," said Job. "Now I see. I repent."

The Lord rebuked Job's first three visitors as false friends, full of folly. They owed the Lord burnt offerings, and Job should pray for them.

Then the Lord made Job wealthy again, with twice as many belongings as before. Job's old friends returned and added to his wealth. Now he had 14,000 sheep, 6,000 cattle, 1,000 pairs of oxen, and 1,000 she donkeys. He had seven more sons and three more beautiful daughters, and Job gave all of them inheritance. Job lived to see his grandchildren and their children—four generations—before he died.

Thus his brutal story ended. Job was left without an explanation for the cruelty shown to him. But he came to an understanding: God is hardly needed for the things we understand; rather, God is essential for all those things we don't understand.

AN ADVERSARY
The wager framing Job's story is between God and an adversary, where the Hebrew term used here is *ha-satan* (השטן). *Satan* means "adversary"—one who opposes your position. Later in the New Testament this word came to mean "devil." The original sense is behind the saying "play devil's advocate." What we have in the tale of Job is a high-stakes wager between God and Satan, with Job being the one to pay the price.

RUTH

When famine came again to Bethlehem a man named Elimelech, his wife Naomi, and their two sons moved to the land of the Moabites. There Elimelech died. Naomi's sons married Moabite women. Ten years passed. Both sons were weak and sickly, and they died, too. Naomi and her daughters-in-law, Orpah and Ruth, were without protection or status, since none of them had husbands or children. Naomi heard that the famine had ended back home, so she told Orpah and Ruth to return to their mothers' homes and marry anew, while she would return to Bethlehem. Orpah and Ruth didn't want to leave Naomi; they followed her.

Naomi insisted, "Turn back." After all, the Moabites had denied the Children of Israel food and water when they were fleeing Egypt. So, by law, Moabites were never accepted into the tribes of Israel. Orpah and Ruth would have better lives in their homeland.

Finally, Orpah kissed Naomi and left. But Ruth clung to Naomi.

"Turn back," said Naomi. Ruth needed her own people, her own home, her own god.

Ruth responded, "Whither you go, I will go. Wherever you lodge, I will lodge. Your people are my people. Your god is my god. Wherever you die, I will die there, too, and be buried there." The two women, joined in a bond of love, returned to Bethlehem.

When they approached the town, the women there said, "Is this Naomi?"

Naomi was taken aback at hearing her name. In that moment it struck her as unsuitable. Her name meant "pleasant," but nothing about her life felt pleasant. She felt the name Mara fit better; that name meant "bitter" and that's how she felt.

It was the time of the barley harvest. When Ruth asked if she could go into the fields to glean—to pick up what the gatherers had

Previous: Naomi belonged to the Children of Israel, though she lived among the Moabites until her husband and sons died. Then she planned to return to Bethlehem alone. But her daughter-in-law Ruth loved her so much, she begged to accompany her.

dropped—Naomi encouraged her. After all, barley grain that the reapers dropped could not be gathered by the owner, but had to be left for the poor, and Naomi and Ruth were poor.

It turned out that Ruth wound up in the field of Boaz, a kinsman of Naomi's dead husband. Boaz said to his reapers, "The Lord be with you"—a friendly greeting. They answered, "The Lord should bless you," a friendly answer. Boaz learned that the new girl was the Moabite daughter-in-law who had returned with Naomi. The reapers told him that she had been diligent all day, gathering the grains and not stopping to rest. Boaz invited Ruth to come every day to glean and drink from his well.

Ruth bowed and asked why he showed such generosity and kindness to a foreigner.

FOOD FESTIVALS
There were three major, weeklong festivals thanking God for food. One began with Passover and marked the beginning of the barley harvest in early spring. The next marked the end of the wheat harvest in early summer. The third marked the end of the fruit harvest and of the agricultural year in general, in autumn. Women were as active in these festivals as men. So they served as general family gatherings, allowing a formal moment to celebrate such things as births and the weaning of children.

"I know you left your birthplace, your mother and father's home—you gave up all you knew for your mother-in-law. May the Lord reward you." Perhaps he was thinking of stories about Abraham, and how the Lord had told Abraham to give up all he knew, for he used the words that the Lord had said to Abraham.

At mealtime, Boaz told Ruth to eat the bread and dip it in the vinegar. He told the reapers to leave extra grain for Ruth. That night Ruth carried home an enormous quantity of barley sheaves. Naomi told Ruth to go back to Boaz's field day after day.

The harvest ended and Naomi and Ruth had enough stored to get them through the winter. But before they could rest, the threshing began. Threshing was a time of celebration. Naomi told Ruth to bathe, dress nice, and go to Boaz after his evening meal. Romance was on her

mind. Perhaps Boaz would marry Ruth. After all, when a man died, often a kinsman took the widow as his own wife. Such a man was called a redeeming kinsman. Since Boaz was a kinsman of Naomi's dead husband Elimelech, that meant he was a kinsman of Ruth.

Ruth did as Naomi said. When Boaz found a girl beside him that night, he asked, "Who are you?"

"I am Ruth, and you are my kinsman, a redeeming kinsman."

"You are kind to choose me instead of a younger man. I am ready to be a redeeming kinsman. But there is another kinsman closer to Elimelech than me. If he will not take you as his wife, I will." Boaz filled Ruth's shawl with six shares of barley.

Boaz went to this other kinsman and explained that he could redeem the land of Naomi's dead husband Elimelech if he wanted. The kinsman agreed. Boaz added that he must also marry Ruth. At that, the kinsman changed his mind. He stood in public and took off his sandal as a symbol of refusing to redeem. So Boaz claimed all of Elimelech's family land and claimed Ruth as his wife.

Soon Ruth and Boaz were blessed with a son. His name was Obed, and he was the father of Jesse, who was the father of David. Yes, the David who would conquer Goliath and become king of a united Israel. So this was a momentous marriage.

Maybe Naomi sensed that. Ruth was a Moabite—one of those viewed as tainted by an instance of corruption ages earlier, in the family of Lot. But Boaz was tainted, too, by an instance of trickery 10 generations earlier, in the family of Jacob-Israel. Ruth and Boaz were good and decent people, but their troubled ancestry could have ruined them. Maybe Naomi sensed that none of that past mattered. What mattered was loyalty, love, kindness, and charity. Those were virtues Ruth showed Naomi and Boaz showed Ruth. Those were virtues that went down through the next four generations to King David. Maybe the Lord chose David to be king because of those virtues.

Boaz, a kinsman of Naomi's husband and therefore of Ruth, owned fields of grain, which Ruth gleaned. With generosity and kindness, they noticed each other's needs and decided to wed.

ESTHER SAVES HER PEOPLE

BOOK OF ESTHER

ESTHER SAVES HER PEOPLE

King Ahasuerus ruled Persia and Media, with provinces that ranged from Cush in Africa across the Arabian Peninsula and down into India. He liked to show off his wealth, so he invited important people from the provinces to his town of Shushan for 180 days of celebration. In the final week, the king held a banquet. His pavilion was decorated in white linen. Indigo cotton with cords of crimson hung from silver cylinders and marble columns. The couches were gold and silver on a paving of alabaster, marble, mother-of-pearl, and black pearl. Men drank wine from gold vessels. At the same time, his beautiful wife Queen Vashti gave a banquet for the women.

On the last day, the king sent seven men servants to fetch Queen Vashti, so he could show off to everyone how beautiful she was, wearing her royal crown.

Queen Vashti refused.

The king was furious. And not very clever. He asked his law experts what he should do to Queen Vashti for disobeying.

These law experts were no fools. "Queen Vashti has done wrong to all of us!" They thought that if women heard that the queen had gotten away with disobeying her husband, women everywhere might try it.

It was decided that the king should issue a royal decree written in the language of each province: Every man should rule his home. Because the queen had disobeyed, she would no longer be queen.

King Ahasuerus's anger soon subsided and he realized he would miss Queen Vashti. But his servants suggested that province officials gather beautiful young women. The king could take his pick. Our far-from-clever king smiled; a beauty contest! What fun!

Among the beautiful young women was Hadassah, also known as Esther, which sounded like "hidden" in Hebrew. Her cousin Mordecai had sheltered her after her parents died. Mordecai was a Jew, which

was the name for a Hebrew in those days. His great-grandfather had been taken from the land of the Children of Israel to Babylonia by King Nebuchadnezzar. Thus he lived in Shushan.

Lovely Esther was brought to the palace. Mordecai made her promise not to tell that her kin were Jews. Daily, he passed in front of the women's court to see what Esther might need.

This bevy of young women was treated well—or as well as one could treat women snatched from their homes. For six months they were rubbed with oil of myrrh. For six more months they were doused with perfumes. After 12 months, the summoning began. In the evening, one young woman would be called to the king. In the morning she'd go back to the women's house. She could not visit the king again unless he called for her by name.

In the 10th month of the seventh year of King Ahasuerus's reign, it was finally Esther's turn to visit the king. The king was smitten with her. He crowned her and named her queen. He held another banquet—Esther's banquet.

Meanwhile, Mordecai hung around the palace gates. There, he overheard two courtiers plotting to kill the king. The king needed to know, of course! He told Esther, and she promptly told the king. The king had the two courtiers impaled on stakes. All of this was written down in the historical records.

Years later, King Ahasuerus promoted a man named Haman to be leader of his royal advisers. Everyone had to bow to Haman. Mordecai refused. When the king's servants asked why, he said as a Jew he bowed only to God. Haman went wild with anger. Probably no Jews would bow to him. He decided to kill them all.

In the first month of the 12th year of the king's reign, Haman tried to figure out when he should go on this killing spree. He used a form of divination based on chance, called *purim*, to make the decision. He cast lots—like throwing dice: The 12th month, called Adar, would be the right time. Haman told the king, "There are people in your kingdom with their own rules. They don't obey the king's rule. This is dangerous." Haman convinced the king to write a decree to have these people killed. He offered to pay for the deed. The king gave Haman his royal ring and told him to keep his money. The scribes wrote the decree in every language in the empire. Couriers carried the scrolls away. The decree said that in the month Adar on the 13th day every Jew should be killed.

At the news, Mordecai went about rending his clothes. He wore sackcloth, threw ashes on his head, and wept. All the Jews did the same. When Esther learned that Mordecai was wearing sackcloth, she had garments brought to him. Mordecai refused to wear them. He sent her a copy of the decree, so she would plead with the king not to kill the Jews. But Esther feared going to the king without being summoned. And it seemed—after five years of marriage—that Esther wasn't in the king's favor, for he hadn't called her to him for 30 days. Mordecai answered, "Perhaps you have risen to this position of power just so you could help in a time like this."

SANCTIONED RECKLESSNESS
Purim is a spring festival of feasting and rejoicing, after a minor fast. During Purim everyone dresses up and makes merry. Purim has much in common with the Catholic festival of Carnival, which precedes a major period of fasting and deprivation called Lent (parallel perhaps to Passover's abstinence from leaven). During Carnival people dress up, make merry, and often do things they wouldn't otherwise, without fear of criticism—sometimes even foolish things. Purim and Carnival affirm the right to be reckless now and then.

Esther told Mordecai to have the Jews of Shushan fast for three days. She and her maidservants would fast, too. Then she'd plead with the king. "If I am lost, I am lost."

After three days, Esther dressed in royal garb and stood in the throne room entrance. The king sat on his throne. When he saw Esther's glowing beauty, he held out his scepter and she touched the tip. "What's troubling you, my queen? What do you need?"

"I have prepared a banquet for Haman," said Esther. "Come and bring him along."

The king and Haman went to drink wine at Esther's banquet. The king again asked her what she wanted.

"Come to another banquet tomorrow, and I'll tell you."

The king's new wife, Esther, invited him and his chief adviser Haman to a banquet, at which she secretly planned to expose Haman's decision to kill all the Jews.

Haman went home happy. On the way he passed Mordecai, who, of course, did not bow to him. When Haman got home, he told everyone how the king and queen respected him. Nevertheless, that fellow Mordecai ruined his pleasure. His friends suggested Haman set up a stake 50 cubits high and impale Mordecai there. Haman set up the stake. He waited outside the palace for dawn, when he could ask the king for permission to impale Mordecai.

That night King Ahasuerus tossed and turned. He had an attendant open the historical records and read to him to lull him to sleep. But, what! The king heard about an event years ago: A certain Mordecai had told Esther about a plot to kill him. The king had forgotten. "What did we do to reward Mordecai?" he asked.

"Nothing."

The king was never clever, but he recognized injustice. He looked outside and saw Haman. He had him fetched. "What should be done for a man the king wants to honor?"

Haman thought the king was talking about him! Wonderful! "Let him wear clothing you have worn and parade through the square riding a horse you have ridden."

"Do this to Mordecai the Jew, who is outside the gate."

Haman did that, then went home for the rest of the day and complained. His advisers and his wife saw no good ahead. But before Haman could figure out what to do, a king's servant fetched him for Esther's second banquet that night.

At that banquet, the king again asked what Esther wanted. She told him her people were about to be destroyed. The king asked who would do such a dastardly thing. Esther pointed. "The evil Haman." The king stormed out of the pavilion. Cringing, Haman went to the queen's couch to beg for mercy. When the king returned, he thought Haman was romancing his queen.

A servant pointed out to the king the tall stake outside. The king had Haman impaled on it.

The king took back the ring he had given to Haman and gave it to Mordecai, for Esther had told him how Mordecai had raised her as his own.

"But you must do more," said Esther. Surely the king had to withdraw his decree.

But a written decree cannot be revoked. The king told Esther and Mordecai to make whatever clever new decree they wanted and seal it with his ring.

In the third month on the 23rd day, Esther and Mordecai made a decree that gave the Jews the right to assemble, defend themselves, and take the spoils of those they conquered.

It wasn't a perfect solution. But Mordecai was happy. And Jews throughout the provinces rejoiced.

On that fated day—in the 12th month on the 13th day—there were battles. The Jews won. But they didn't take spoils. Maybe they were repenting. For Mordecai was in the family of Saul, the first king, who had kept the beasts of the Amalekites even after the Lord had told him to destroy them. And Haman was in the family of the Amalekites. The Jews were obeying the Lord's original demand.

The king rewarded Mordecai for saving his life years before by having him wear clothing the king himself had worn and parading through the square on a horse the king himself had ridden.

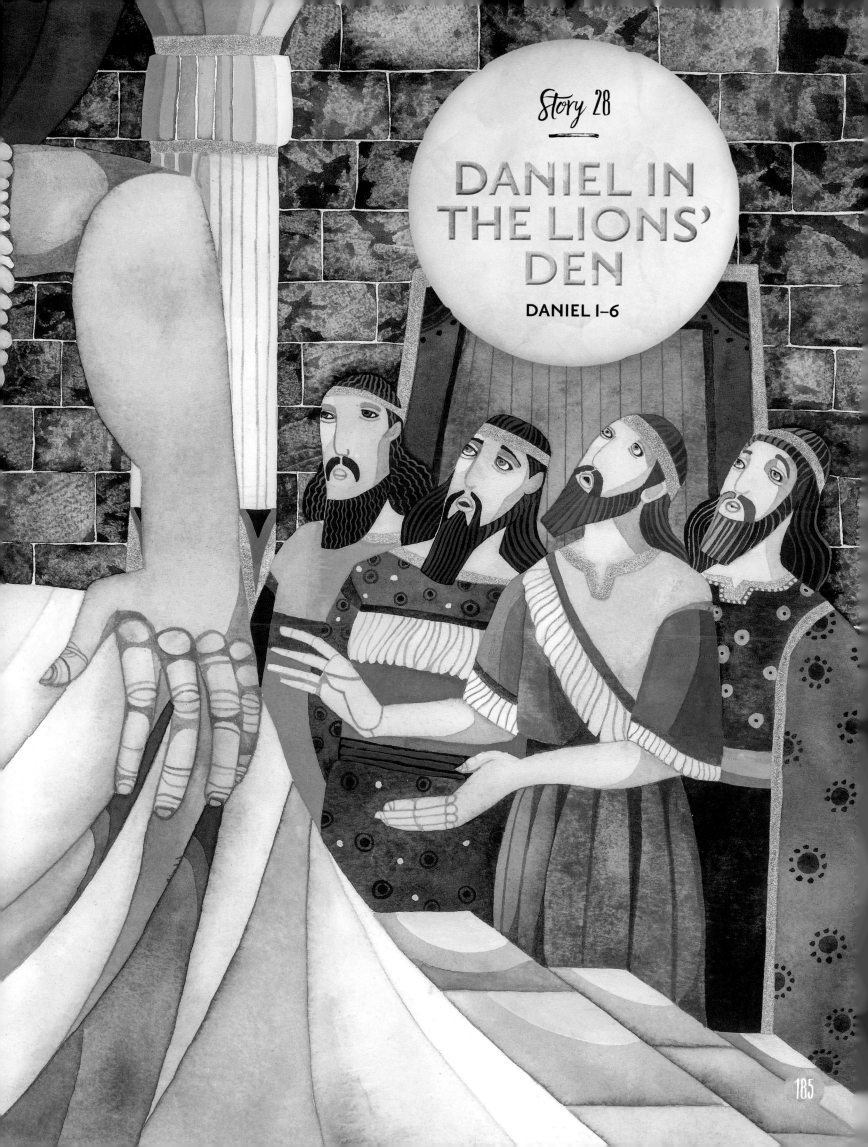

DANIEL IN THE LIONS' DEN

King Nebuchadnezzar of Babylonia lay siege on Jerusalem and won. He plundered the glorious temple that Solomon had built, bringing home the finest vessels to put in his own god's house. He ordered that the smartest and best-looking of the young men among the Children of Israel should be whisked off to Babylonia to educate the Babylonians. The king planned to spend three years preparing these men to serve him, teaching them to speak and read Babylonian languages so they could do their job properly.

Among these best and brightest were four friends: Daniel, Hananiah, Mishael, and Azariah. Each was given a Babylonian name. Daniel, which meant "as God is my judge," was renamed Belteshazzar. Hananiah became Shadrach, Mishael became Meshach, and Azariah became Abednego. If renaming was supposed to integrate them into the new culture, it didn't work: Daniel refused to eat the food or drink the wine of the king, since it went against his religion. The servant in charge of these young men liked Daniel and he worried that Daniel's health would fail. Daniel decided to allay the man's worries by offering a test. For 10 days he and his three friends ate only grains and lentils and drank only water. At the end of 10 days, they were plumper and healthier than those who ate the king's fare. The man was convinced; the four Children of Israel were allowed to eat as they wished.

These four friends learned fast and grew wise. Daniel came to understand dreams and visions, like Joseph had years before. King Nebuchadnezzar found these four to be 10 times wiser than his wizards and soothsayers.

One day the king had a terrifying dream. He called together wise men to interpret it, among them, these four Children of Israel. They asked, "So, what was this dream?" The king wouldn't tell; the wise men must discern the dream on their own. That way the king would be sure that they interpreted it properly. The wise men protested; no one could do that. King Nebuchadnezzar ordered his sages put to death, including the new young Children of Israel.

Daniel asked the king to give him time to figure out the dream. Then he had a night vision. Afterward he praised the Lord "who rules the days and seasons, who lifts up kings and brings them down, who gives wisdom to the wise, knows the mysteries of the darkness, and dwells in light." He asked to be brought before the king.

The king asked, "Can you explain my dream?"

"In your dream you saw a colossal statue. Its head was gold; its chest and arms, silver; its loins and thighs, bronze; its legs, iron; its feet, part iron and part clay. You saw a stone, hurled out of the blue, shatter those feet. The statue crumbled. The stone grew into a mountain that filled the earth. This is what it means. You are the mightiest king—so you are the gold head. Next will come an inferior kingdom of silver, then a more inferior one of bronze, and finally a kingdom of iron that will shatter the empire, like that rock shattered the statue. That fourth kingdom will not hold together, since clay and iron don't hold together. God will make another kingdom that will be strong and will endure forever."

The grateful king made Daniel governor over the sages, like what had happened to Joseph when he interpreted Pharaoh's dream that portended seven years of prosperity followed by seven years of famine. Daniel asked that his three friends be made sages, too.

The king had a gold statue built, 60 cubits high, 6 cubits wide. He had his herald announce that whenever the people heard the horn, bagpipe, lute, zither, lyre, flute, and all

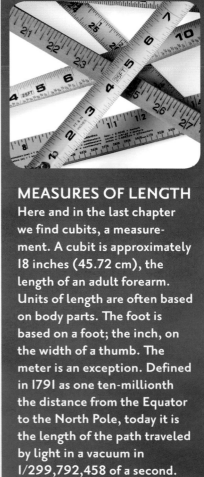

MEASURES OF LENGTH
Here and in the last chapter we find cubits, a measurement. A cubit is approximately 18 inches (45.72 cm), the length of an adult forearm. Units of length are often based on body parts. The foot is based on a foot; the inch, on the width of a thumb. The meter is an exception. Defined in 1791 as one ten-millionth the distance from the Equator to the North Pole, today it is the length of the path traveled by light in a vacuum in 1/299,792,458 of a second.

kinds of music, they must drop down and worship the king's gold statue or be thrown into a fiery furnace. The Children of Israel, though, wouldn't worship the statue; it was against their religion.

The king called forth Daniel's three friends. (Where Daniel was right then, no one knows.) He'd burn them up if they didn't obey. The friends refused. The king had a fiery furnace prepared, seven times hotter than usual. It was so hot that those servants who threw the three friends into the fire burned up themselves.

The king jumped up in astonishment. "What? I see four men walking in the fire. The fourth looks divine." He called out to the three he had seen thrown in, each by name. "Come out!" Those three came out, unsinged, unharmed. The king declared that their God was true.

Years later, when Nebuchadnezzar's son Belshazzar was king, he held a feast. In a drunken stupor, he and his friends drank from the gold and silver vessels that Nebuchadnezzar had stolen from the temple in Jerusalem. Bad mistake! A disembodied hand appeared and wrote on the palace wall. King Belshazzar's face went dark, his loins went slack, his knees hammered. He called out, "Whoever can interpret this

writing shall wear royal purple and have a golden collar and rule a third of the kingdom." But no one could do it. The queen spoke of Daniel, who had a reputation for interpreting dreams.

Daniel said he didn't want a robe or collar or part of the kingdom. He would interpret the writing out of respect for old Nebuchadnezzar, Belshazzar's father. King Nebuchadnezzar had started out good—Daniel remembered that—but the king had become haughty as he grew mighty and wound up being turned out by God like a beast, to live among the wild donkeys and chew the grass, until he finally became humble. "You, King Belshazzar," said Daniel, "you saw this happen to your father. You should have known better. You should have been humble." Instead, the young King Belshazzar had drunk from the holy vessels.

Daniel read what the Lord had written on the wall. "*Mene mene teqal ufarsin*—those are the words. *Mene* means 'count'—your days are numbered. *Teqal* means the weight of the money 'shekel'—you have been weighed. *Ufarsin* has within it the sound of *peras*, which means 'break apart'—your kingdom has been broken."

Whenever the people heard music, they were to bow down in worship to the gold statue. But the four Children of Israel in the king's employ refused. So the king had three of them thrown into a fiery furnace. Somehow four appeared there, unharmed—one divine in appearance.

King Darius' officers threw Daniel into the lions' den because he refused to stop praying. But when the king went to check the next morning, Daniel was sitting, safe and whole, among the close-mouthed lions.

The astonished Belshazzar clothed Daniel in royal purple with a gold collar and gave him rule over one third of the kingdom.

That night the king was slain.

Darius, a Mede, became the next king, a good king. He made Daniel one of three overseers of the officers. Daniel did so well, that the king thought of promoting him to top overseer. That sparked jealousy among the others. The officers tried to find a way to bring down Daniel. But Daniel seemed to have no flaws. They had to trap him— and the best trap was through his religion.

They told the king, "You should issue a binding edict that for 30 days anyone who petitions any god or man other than you will be thrown into the lions' den."

King Darius had the edict put in writing.

Daniel prayed to God three times a day, as always. Of course, the officers denounced Daniel to King Darius.

King Darius cared for Daniel. He searched for a way to spare him. But a binding edict cannot be revoked. The officers threw Daniel into the lions' den and pushed a huge stone over the mouth of the den.

That night the king couldn't eat. He couldn't sleep. At dawn he rushed to the lions' den and shouted to Daniel.

What do you know, Daniel answered. He was alive! "Oh, King, live forever. God's messengers shut the lions' jaws."

Darius saw this as proof that Daniel was blameless before God and king. Darius ordered Daniel's enemies thrown into the lions' den. His next edict told the people to fear and tremble before the true God, Daniel's God.

Thus did the Children of Israel prosper in the time of Darius. In the time of Cyrus, who followed Darius, they built the second temple in Jerusalem, to replace Solomon's, which King Nebuchadnezzar had plundered.

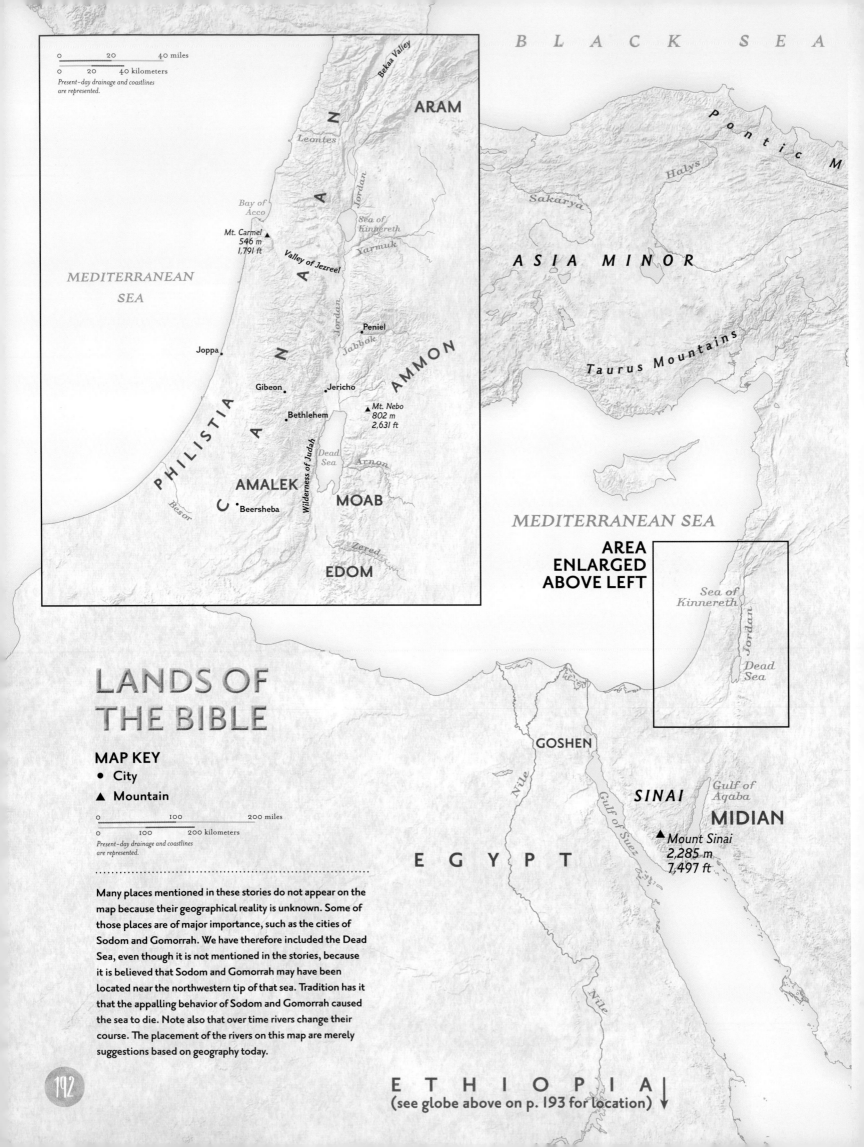

B L A C K S E A

P o n t i c M

ARAM

Leontes

Z

Bekaa Valley

Bay of Acco

Mt. Carmel ▲
546 m
1,791 ft

Valley of Jezreel

A

N

A

A

C

Jordan

Sea of Kinnereth

Yarmuk

Sakarya

Halys

ASIA MINOR

Taurus Mountains

Joppa

Gibeon

Jericho

Bethlehem

• Peniel

Jabbok

AMMON

Mt. Nebo ▲
802 m
2,631 ft

MEDITERRANEAN SEA

Jordan

PHILISTIA

Besor

AMALEK

• Beersheba

C

Wilderness of Judah

Dead Sea

Arnon

MOAB

EDOM

Zered

MEDITERRANEAN SEA

AREA
ENLARGED
ABOVE LEFT

Sea of Kinnereth

Jordan

Dead Sea

scale:
0   20   40 miles
0   20   40 kilometers

Present-day drainage and coastlines are represented.

LANDS OF
THE BIBLE

MAP KEY
● City
▲ Mountain

0   100   200 miles
0   100   200 kilometers

Present-day drainage and coastlines are represented.

Many places mentioned in these stories do not appear on the map because their geographical reality is unknown. Some of those places are of major importance, such as the cities of Sodom and Gomorrah. We have therefore included the Dead Sea, even though it is not mentioned in the stories, because it is believed that Sodom and Gomorrah may have been located near the northwestern tip of that sea. Tradition has it that the appalling behavior of Sodom and Gomorrah caused the sea to die. Note also that over time rivers change their course. The placement of the rivers on this map are merely suggestions based on geography today.

GOSHEN

Nile

Gulf of Suez

Gulf of Aqaba

SINAI

MIDIAN

▲ Mount Sinai
2,285 m
7,497 ft

E G Y P T

Nile

E T H I O P I A ↓
(see globe above on p. 193 for location)

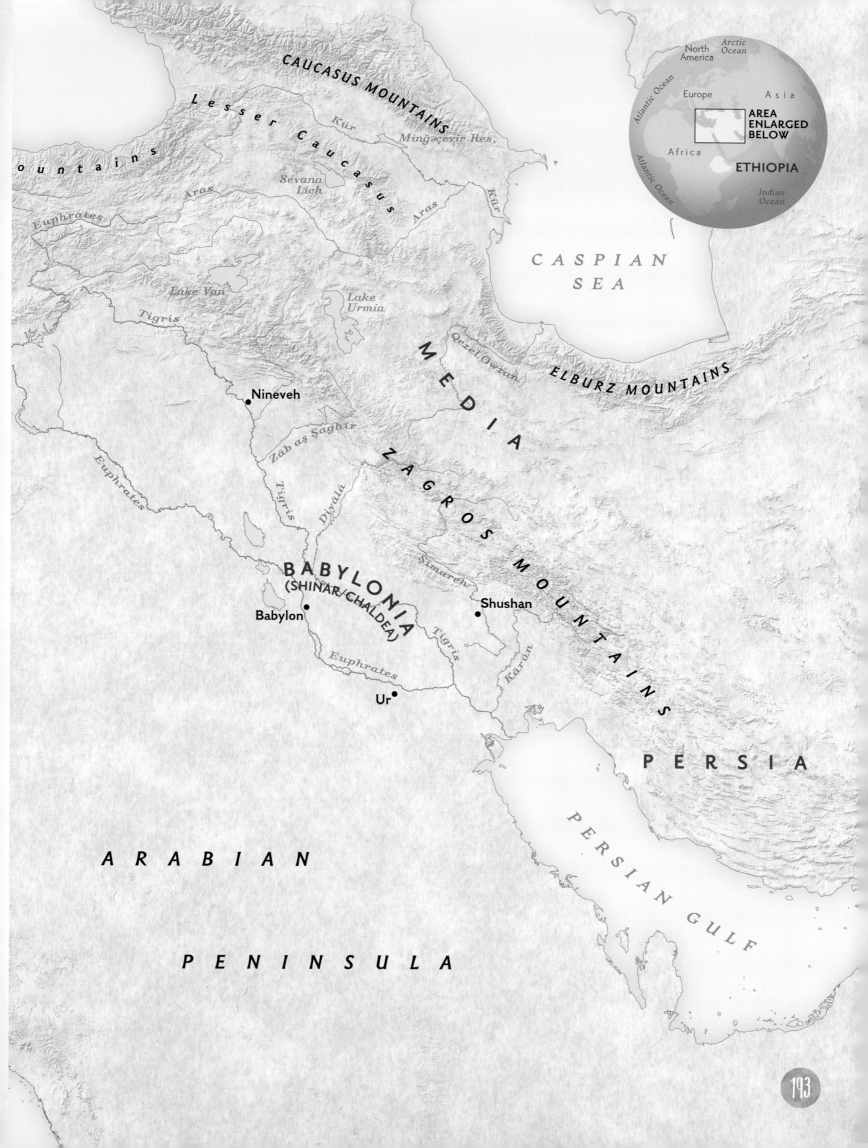

CAUCASUS MOUNTAINS

Lesser Caucasus

ountains

Kür

Mingəçevir Res.

Aras

Sevana
Lich

Aras

Kür

Euphrates

Lake Van

Lake
Urmia

Tigris

North
America

Arctic
Ocean

Europe

Asia

Atlantic Ocean

AREA
ENLARGED
BELOW

Africa

Atlantic
Ocean

ETHIOPIA

Indian
Ocean

CASPIAN
SEA

M
E
D
I
A

Qezel Owzan

ELBURZ MOUNTAINS

Nineveh

Zāb aş Şaghīr

Z
A
G
R
O
S

M
O
U
N
T
A
I
N
S

Tigris

Diyālá

BABYLONIA
(SHINAR/CHALDEA)

Simareh

Babylon

Shushan

Tigris

Euphrates

Kārūn

Ur

P E R S I A

A R A B I A N

PERSIAN

P E N I N S U L A

GULF

193

TIMELINE
of Early Civilizations in the Near East and Bordering Areas*

10,000–8000 B.C.E.

The earliest building we have evidence of is in southeast Turkey. It is believed to have served as an enormous sanctuary for periodic meetings of people who probably came from far and wide.

Circa 9300 B.C.E.

Early village farming communities gradually popped up here and there. One of the earliest was to the north of Jericho, where people cultivated wild emmer (a kind of wheat).

9000–7000 B.C.E.

Sheep were domesticated in Mesopotamia, between the Euphrates and Tigris Rivers, giving a reliable source of milk, meat, and wool.

Circa 8500 B.C.E.

The now extinct cattle known as aurochs were domesticated in southeast Turkey. They were believed to have been aggressive and large (standing nearly a foot taller than modern large cattle).

8400–8100 B.C.E.

Human settlements pop up all across the south of Turkey.

*This timeline mentions the names of farming areas and cities of ancient times as well as modern place-names.

Circa 8000 B.C.E.

The bezoar ibex, a kind of goat, was domesticated in Iran.

Emmer, durum, and einkorn wheat were domesticated in Ethiopia, Syria, and Turkey.

7000 B.C.E.

A large agricultural settlement was built in northern Iraq.

7000–4000 B.C.E.

Pottery was fired to the southwest of Nineveh.

The potter's wheel was invented in Mesopotamia.

6000–4300 B.C.E.

Sailboats were first used in Mesopotamia.

6000 B.C.E.

Irrigation (supplying water to farmland) was used in Mesopotamia and Egypt.

5500 B.C.E.

Large-scale agriculture began in the south of Mesopotamia. The same happened along the Nile River.

5100 B.C.E.

Mesopotamians built temples to the gods.

4500 B.C.E.

Cities grew up in the Shushan area and along the Nile River.

4000 B.C.E.

Wooden plows were used in Mesopotamia, speeding up the rate at which fields could be tilled and increasing the number and kinds of areas that could be planted.

Egyptians made bread using yeast for the first time, gradually revolutionizing the way bread would be made across the world.

The wild African ass was domesticated in Egypt and Mesopotamia, leading to donkeys.

They became the most important carriers of humans and other loads, and they helped in agriculture.

The city of Ur was founded.

3500–3000 B.C.E.

Wheeled vehicles were used in Mesopotamia. This invention changed the history of humankind, ranging from agriculture to travel to machines of various types.

Cities formed in Egypt.

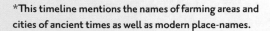

3300 B.C.E.

Earliest hieroglyphics appeared in Egypt. These were largely pre-writing forms, used for keeping records (of taxes, for example) but not for telling narratives (a written account of events).

3100 B.C.E.

Upper and Lower Egyptian Kingdoms united into the first large nation in the world.

3000 B.C.E.

Sumerians developed the cuneiform writing style of wedge-shaped symbols. Before this, the marks in clay were mostly pictorial. At this point, cuneiform writing changed to narratives that reflected spoken languages.

Dromedaries, one-humped camels, were domesticated in Somalia and southern Arabia and used mostly for transportation.

2560 B.C.E.

The Great Pyramid at Giza was completed.

2500 B.C.E.

Camels were domesticated in central Asia.

The Assyrians in Mesopotamia, in the areas that are now northern Iraq and southeastern Turkey, were so organized in their system of government and commerce that some archaeologists call them a state.

2334–2154 B.C.E.

The Akkadian Empire thrived in Mesopotamia.

2300–300 B.C.E.

Canaanites, also known as Phoenicians, were a mix of indigenous settled and nomadic groups that inhabited the Eastern Mediterranean coast. Their languages formed a family (the Semitic family), the only surviving daughter today being Hebrew. From 1600 to 1360 much of Canaanite land was an Egyptian colony. They invented the world's first alphabet, which gradually replaced cuneiform writing. From about 1500 to 500 B.C.E. this civilization spread across the Mediterranean, bringing their alphabet with them.

2111–2004 B.C.E.

The Third Dynasty of Ur, the last Sumerian dynasty in Mesopotamia, was in this period. The Elamites destroyed Ur in 2004 B.C.E.

2052–1570 B.C.E.

Middle Kingdom in Egypt.

2004–1763 B.C.E.

The Ammonites established city-states in Mesopotamia.

TIMELINE

1830–1531 B.C.E.

Babylon (an Akkadian-speaking city) became an empire in 1830 B.C.E. and was finally sacked in 1531. After that point, the city was under the rule of many other groups of people, including the Assyrians and the Elamites. The sixth king of the First Dynasty was Hammurabi, famous for establishing a set of law codes that detailed penalties for crimes, known as the Code of Hammurabi.

1600–1200 B.C.E.

Hittites established an empire in Turkey that spread south into Mesopotamia and somewhat along the coast. They struggled with the Egyptian Empire and the Middle Assyrian Empire, and eventually the Assyrians took over much of their land, while the Phrygians took over the rest.

1500–1077 B.C.E.

New Kingdom in Egypt.

1366–609 B.C.E.

The Middle Assyrian Empire was established in 1366 B.C.E. It grew enormously. From 911 on, it is known as the Neo-Assyrian Empire. It was the largest empire of the world, spanning across the ancient Near East (Western Asia) into the Arabian Peninsula and North Africa.

1300 B.C.E.

This was the start of the Iron Age, with iron smelting (heating and melting) in Turkey. The Assyrians were the first people to use iron weapons, which helped their empire grow.

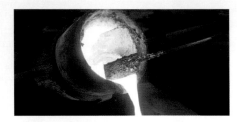

1279–1213 B.C.E.

Pharaoh Ramses II ruled Egypt. In the ancient capital city of Pi-Ramses, on the Nile Delta, there was a dramatic climate shift from warm and wet to dry. Scientists speculate that the Nile current, which had been rapid, now turned slow. The river became muddy and thick with algae. If this happened, many creatures would have been affected and some might have died in great numbers, including frogs. The population of insects, such as flies, mosquitoes, and lice, would have grown rapidly, and could have caused diseases in livestock and boils on people.

Additionally, on the Greek island of Santorini, one of the biggest volcanic eruptions in history took place. The air around the eastern half of the Mediterranean Sea would have been full of ash, causing hail and darkness and even locusts.

Some scholars argue that these two natural disasters coincide with the 10 plagues when Moses led the Children of Israel out of Egypt.

Circa 1020–980 B.C.E.

King David of the Hebrew Bible might well have been a monarch during this period.

722 B.C.E.

Assyria conquers the northern kingdom of Israel.

620–539 B.C.E.

Nebuchadnezzar's father established a dynasty in Babylon in 620 B.C.E. Nebuchadnezzar ascended to the throne in 605 B.C.E. and managed to expand the kingdom to include Phoenicia and various Assyrian provinces.

600 B.C.E.

The Babylonian calendar was devised, based on 12 cycles of the moon (known as lunar cycles).

586 B.C.E.

Babylon conquers Judea and destroys the temple, and exiles Israelites to Babylon.

539 B.C.E.

Persia conquers Babylon and allows the Israelites to return and rebuild the temple.

THE PEOPLE OF THE BIBLE

ADAM

Book of the Bible: Created in Genesis 2:7 and is a figure through his long life, which ends in Genesis 5:5.

Known for: Being the first man, the husband of Eve, and the father of Cain, Abel, and Seth.

EVE

Book of the Bible: Created in Genesis 2:22, from Adam's rib. There is no mention of her after Genesis 4:1.

Known for: Eating forbidden fruit from the Tree of Knowledge in the Garden of Eden. She was the first woman, wife of Adam, mother of Cain, Abel, and Seth.

CAIN

Book of the Bible: Appears in Genesis 4:1 and mentioned last in Genesis 4:17.

Known for: Being the first son of Adam and Eve and slaying his younger brother Abel out of jealousy.

ABEL

Book of the Bible: Appears in Genesis 4:2 and is killed in Genesis 4:8 by his older brother.

Known for: Being the second son of Adam and Eve and taking care of animals.

NOAH

Book of the Bible: Appears in Genesis 5:29 and dies in Genesis 9:29.

Known for: Finding favor in the eyes of the Lord, when other humans did not. Noah, his wife, and his three sons with their wives built the ark that saved humankind, land creatures, and fowl from the flood.

ABRAM (ABRAHAM)

Book of the Bible: He appears in Genesis 11:26, has his name changed to Abraham in Genesis 17:5, and dies in Genesis 25:8.

Known for: Being told by the Lord to go to Canaan and prosper. Also, for being told that his descendants would suffer in another country, but emerge triumphant.

SARAI (SARAH)

Book of the Bible: Appears in Genesis 11:29, has her changed to Sarah in Genesis 17:15, and dies in Genesis 23:2.

Known for: Being the wife of Abraham and the mother of Isaac. She was buried in a cave in Canaan.

LOT

Book of the Bible: Appears in Genesis 11:31. The last we hear of him is in Genesis 19.

Known for: The fate of his wife, who turned to a pillar of salt because she disobeyed the Lord and looked back as they fled the burning cities of Sodom and Gomorrah.

THE PEOPLE OF THE BIBLE

HAGAR

Book of the Bible: Appears in Genesis 16:1 and the last we see of her is in Genesis 21:21.

Known for: Being the Egyptian servant of Sarah, and the mother of Abraham's first child, Ishmael. Abraham sent her off into the desert with Ishmael after his son Isaac was born.

ISHMAEL

Book of the Bible: Appears in Genesis 16:15 and is last seen in Genesis 25:17.

Known for: Being brought into the desert by his mother, then living far away. After the death of his father Abraham, he and his brother Isaac buried their father together. His 12 sons became tribal leaders.

ISAAC

Book of the Bible: First mentioned in Genesis 17:21. He is born in Genesis 21:2 and dies in Genesis 35:29.

Known for: Almost being sacrificed by his father Abraham, but being rescued by an angel of the Lord. He married Rebekah and had twin sons: Esau and Jacob.

ELIEZER

Book of the Bible: First mentioned in Genesis 15:2. We assume he is the senior servant of Abraham mentioned in Genesis 24:2. He appears throughout Genesis 24.

Known for: Being sent to the land of Abraham's birth to find a wife for Isaac. He brought back Rebekah, Isaac's cousin.

REBEKAH

Book of the Bible: First mentioned in Genesis 22:23. She appears in Genesis 24:15. The last we see of her is in Genesis 27.

Known for: Eliezer taking her back to Canaan to marry Isaac, with whom she had twin sons, Esau and Jacob. Also, for helping Jacob trick Isaac.

ESAU

Book of the Bible: Born in Genesis 25:25. Appears in Genesis 33 and Genesis 36.

Known for: Being the older twin to Jacob. He had the rights of the first son, and he was his father Isaac's favorite. But Jacob tricked Isaac into giving Esau's birthright blessing to Jacob.

JACOB-ISRAEL

Book of the Bible: Born in Genesis 25:26 and dies in Genesis 49:33. His name is changed to Israel in Genesis 35:10.

Known for: Being Esau's twin brother and his mother Rebekah's favorite. Also, for tricking Esau out of his birthright and fathering a daughter and the leaders of the tribes of Israel.

RACHEL

Book of the Bible: Appears in Genesis 29:6. She dies after giving birth to a second son in Genesis 35:19.

Known for: Being the mother of Joseph and the second wife of Jacob.

LEAH

Book of the Bible: First appears in Genesis 29:16. We learn in Genesis 49:31 that Jacob buried her in Canaan.

Known for: Being Rachel's older sister and Jacob's first wife. She gave Jacob his first son, Reuben. In all, she had six sons and Jacob's only daughter, Dinah.

JOSEPH

Book of the Bible: Born in Genesis 30:23 and dies in Genesis 50:26.

Known for: Being Rachel's first son and Jacob-Israel's favorite son; Jacob made him a beautiful robe. Joseph interpreted the dreams of Pharaoh and saved Egypt from starvation during a famine.

MOSES

Book of the Bible: Born in Exodus 2:2 and dies in Deuteronomy 34:5.

Known for: Being found as an infant in a basket on the Nile by the pharaoh's daughter. Moses also carved the stone tablets with the Commandments. He brought the Children of Israel to the land where Jericho was.

JOSHUA

Book of the Bible: First appears in Exodus 17:9 and dies in Joshua 24:29.

Known for: Being Moses' assistant, sent to scout out Canaan. After Moses' death, he led the people to conquer Jericho, and then to conquer surrounding lands, which he distributed among the Children of Israel.

SAMSON

Book of the Bible: Born in Judges 13:24 and dies in Judges 16:30.

Known for: Being exceptionally strong. He strangled a lion and was the leader of the Children of Israel for 20 years. But his wife Delilah betrayed him, telling the Philistines how to make him weak.

DAVID

Book of the Bible: First mentioned in 1 Samuel 16:1. He dies in 1 Kings 2:10.

Known for: Being a small shepherd and musician who killed the large man Goliath with a stone. He became the second king of the Children of Israel, waging war against the house of the first king.

GOLIATH

Book of the Bible: First appears in 1 Samuel 17:4 and is killed in 1 Samuel 17:49-50.

Known for: Challenging the Children of Israel to present someone to fight with him to determine which people would rule over the other. The boy David killed him with a stone.

SAUL

Book of the Bible: First mentioned in 1 Samuel 9:2 and dies in 1 Samuel 31:4.

Known for: Being anointed by the prophet Samuel as the first king of the Children of Israel. He made David a battlefield leader and then turned on him and waged war.

THE PEOPLE OF THE BIBLE

SOLOMON

Book of the Bible: Born in 2 Samuel 12:24 and dies in 1 Kings 11:43.

Known for: Being the wise second son of King David and Bathsheba, and the third king of the Children of Israel.

ELIJAH

Book of the Bible: First appears in 1 Kings 17:1, and leaves the earth in 2 Kings 2:11.

Known for: Being loyal to the Lord, when the other prophets had left the faith. People of all faiths turned against him. The Lord brought him up to the heavens in a whirlwind.

ELISHA

Book of the Bible: First appears in 1 Kings 19:16, and dies of illness in 2 Kings 13:14.

Known for: Being the disciple of the prophet Elijah, performing miracles, and being a healer.

JONAH

Book of the Bible: The main person in the Book of Jonah.

Known for: Running away when the Lord told him to go to Nineveh and preach against the wickedness there. He fled on a ship and was thrown overboard and swallowed by a huge fish.

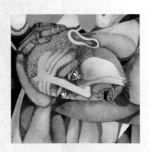

JOB

Book of the Bible: The main person in the Book of Job.

Known for: Suffering terribly because of a wager the Lord had with the adversary. Job loses his property and then his children, and yet he stays faithful. But when he has personal pain, he questions why.

NAOMI

Book of the Bible: One of the two main people in the Book of Ruth.

Known for: Being the mother-in-law of Ruth. Naomi and her husband had moved to Moab. But her husband and sons died. She returned to Bethlehem, and one of her daughters-in-law, Ruth, accompanied her.

RUTH

Book of the Bible: The main person in the Book of Ruth.

Known for: Loving her mother-in-law Naomi so much that she abandoned her home and religion and went with Naomi to live among the Children of Israel. She remarried and had a son Obed, who had a son Jesse, who had a son David—the second king.

BOAZ

Book of the Bible: Appears in Ruth 2–4.

Known for: Being the second husband of Ruth. Boaz was a relative of Naomi's late husband and a landowner. He was kind to the widows and fell in love with Ruth and married her.

MORDECAI

Book of the Bible: Appears in Esther 2 and throughout the rest of Esther.

Known for: Being the cousin of Esther, who raised her and helped her save the Jews from the decree that would kill them.

HAMAN

Book of the Bible: Appears in Esther 3:1 and is killed in Esther 7:10.

Known for: Hating the Jews because they would not bow down to anyone but their God. He got the king to sign a decree that all the Jews should be killed.

KING NEBUCHADNEZZAR

Book of the Bible: Appears in Daniel 1–4.

Known for: Being the king of Babylon, who had men from the Jewish nobility brought to his palace to learn Babylonian and then serve in his court. Among them was Daniel, who interpreted the king's dream correctly.

DANIEL

Book of the Bible: The main person of the Book of Daniel.

Known for: Interpreting the dream of King Nebuchadnezzar, interpreting the writing on the wall for Nebuchadnezzar's son Belshazzar (who was king then), and being thrown into the lions' den by the next king, Darius.

ESTHER

Book of the Bible: The main person in the Book of Esther.

Known for: Becoming queen to King Ahasuerus of Persia and saving her people, the Children of Israel, from a murderous decree. She gets the king to allow the Jews to fight off their enemies.

KING AHASUERUS

Book of the Bible: Appears throughout the Book of Esther.

Known for: Being the king of all Persia and Media. He had many wives and great wealth, and he listened to Esther when she revealed she was Jewish and gave her the permission she requested.

BIBLIOGRAPHY

Stories

Alter, Robert. 2004. *The Five Books of Moses.* New York: Norton.

Alter, Robert. 2010. *The Wisdom Books: Job, Proverbs, and Ecclesiastes.* New York: Norton.

Alter, Robert. 2013. *Ancient Israel: The Former Prophets: Joshua, Samuel, and Kings.* New York: Norton.

Alter, Robert. 2015. *Strong as Death Is Love: The Song of Songs: Ruth, Esther, Jonah, and Daniel.* New York: Norton.

Fox, Everett. 1995. *The Five Books of Moses.* New York: Schocken Books.

Fox, Everett. 1999. *Give Us a King! Samuel, Saul, and David.* New York: Schocken Books.

Fox, Everett. 2014. *The Early Prophets: Joshua, Judges, Samuel, and Kings.* New York: Schocken Books.

Sidebars

"17th General Conference on Weights and Measures (1983), Resolution 1." Available at: bipm.org/en/CGPM/db/17/1/ (Page 187)

Ahrens, C. Donald. 2012. *Meteorology Today: An Introduction to Weather, Climate, and the Environment.* 10th edition. Belmont, CA: Cengage Learning. (Page 39)

Alter, Robert. 2013. *Ancient Israel: The Former Prophets: Joshua, Judges, Samuel, and Kings: A Translation With Commentary.* New York: Norton. (Page 124)

Alter, Robert. 2010. *The Wisdom Books: Job, Proverbs, and Ecclesiastes.* New York: Norton. (Page 169)

Arbib, Michael A. "From Monkey-like Action Recognition to Human Language: An Evolutionary Framework for Neurolinguistics." *Behavioral and Brain Sciences* 28.02 (2005): 105-124. (Page 42)

Bar-Ilan, Meir. *King Solomon's Trade With India.* Aram 27: 1&2 (2015), 125-137. (Page 149)

"Base Unit Definitions: Meter" National Institute of Standards and Technology. Available at: physics.nist.gov/cuu/Units/meter.html (Page 187)

Beal, Timothy K. 2002. *The Book of Hiding: Gender, Ethnicity, Annihilation, and Esther.* Abingdon on Thames, U.K.: Routledge. (Page 179)

Berns, Andrew. "Reckless Rites: Purim and the Legacy of Jewish Violence." *Medieval Encounters* 14.2 (2008): 410-412. (Page 180)

Bickerton, Derek. "Language Evolution: A Brief Guide for Linguists." *Lingua* 117.3 (2007): 510-526. (Page 42)

Bullinger, Ethelbert William. 2006. *Number in Scripture.* New York: Cosimo. (Page 118)

Butzer, Karl W. 1976. *Early Hydraulic Civilization in Egypt: A Study in Cultural Ecology.* Chicago: University of Chicago Press. (Page 94)

Coates, Michael, and Marcello Ruta. "Nice Snake, Shame About the Legs." *Trends in Ecology & Evolution* 15.12 (2000): 503-507. (Page 25)

Davis, William. "The Anatomy of a Whale: Transatlantic Audiences and 'the Good Bishop' Jebb in Moby-Dick." *Leviathan* 18.2 (2016): 53-61. (Page 161)

Dilke, Oswald Ashton Wentworth. 1987. *Mathematics and Measurement.* Vol. 2. London: British Museum Publications. (Page 187)

Dimbleby, Geoffrey W. 2017. *The Domestication and Exploitation of Plants and Animals.* New York: Routledge. (Page 31)

Dozeman, Thomas B. "The Yam-Sûp in the Exodus and the Crossing of the Jordan River." *The Catholic Biblical Quarterly* 58.3 (1996): 407-416. (Page 111)

Ebeling, Jennie R. 2010. *Women's Lives in Biblical Times.* New York: Bloomsbury Publishing. (see particularly chapter one) (Page 173)

Erlacher, Daniel, and Michael Schredl. "Time Required for Motor Activity in Lucid Dreams." *Perceptual and Motor Skills* 99.3 suppl. (2004): 1239-1242. (Page 55)

Finkelstein, Israel. "Arabian Trade and Socio-Political Conditions in the Negev in the Twelfth-Eleventh Centuries B.C.E." *Journal of Near Eastern Studies* 47.4 (1988): 241-252. (Page 149)

Forsyth, Neil. 1989. *The Old Enemy: Satan and the Combat Myth.* Princeton, NJ: Princeton University Press. (Page 169)

Fradkin, Chris, Gelson Vanderlei Weschenfelder, and Maria Angela Mattar Yunes. "Shared Adversities of Children and Comic Super-heroes as Resources for Promoting Resilience." *Child Abuse & Neglect* 51 (2016): 407-415. (Page 129)

Garfinkel, Yosef, and Saar Ganor. "Khirbet Qeiyafa: Shaarayimn." *Journal of Hebrew Scriptures* 8 (2008): 1-10. (Page 135)

Henslow, George. 1895. *The Plants of the Bible.* Vol. 7. London: Religious Tract Society. (Page 83)

Herlihy, David, and Samuel Kline Cohn. 1997. *The Black Death and the Transformation of the West.* Cambridge, MA: Harvard University Press. (Page 49)

Hough, Carole, ed. 2016. *The Oxford Handbook of Names and Naming.* Oxford: Oxford University Press. (Page 75)

Livi-Bacci, Massimo. 2012. *A Concise History of World Population.* Chichester, West Sussex, U.K.: John Wiley & Sons. (Page 49)

Loprieno, Antonio. 1995. *Ancient Egyptian: A Linguistic Introduction.* Cambridge: Cambridge University Press. (Page 89)

News24. 10 June 2014. "Jonah and the Whale Intestines." Available at: news24.com/MyNews24/Jonah-and-the-Whale-Intestines -20140610 (Page 161)

Regenstein, J. M., M. M. Chaudry, and C. E. Regenstein. "The Kosher and Halal Food Laws." *Comprehensive Reviews in Food Science and Food Safety* 2.3 (2003): 111-127. (Page 104)

Rendsburg, Gary A. (n.d.) "Agricultural Origins of the Jewish Holidays." Accessed May 13, 2017: http://hazon.org/wp-content/uploads/2011/08/Agricultural-Origins-of-the-Jewish-Holidays.pdf (Page 124)

Rendsburg, Gary A. 1998. "The Early History of Israel." In *Crossing Boundaries and Linking Horizons: Studies in Honor of Michael C. Astour on His 80th Birthday,* eds. Gordon D. Young and Mark W. Chavalas, 433-453. Potomac, MD: Capital Decisions. (Page 173)

Sabaté, Joan. "Religion, Diet and Research." *The British Journal of Nutrition* 92.2 (2004): 199-201. (Page 104)

Said, Rushdi. 2013. *The River Nile: Geology, Hydrology and Utilization.* Elsevier. (Page 94)

Sapir-Hen, Lidar, and Erez Ben-Yosef. "The Introduction of Domestic Camels to the Southern Levant: Evidence From the Aravah Valley." *Tel Aviv* 40.2 (2013): 277-285. (Page 61)

Schram, Peninnah. 1991. *Tales of Elijah the Prophet.* Northvale, NJ: Jason Aronson. (Page 155)

Tacci, Jennifer. 2016. "Apocalypses and Superhero Mythology." In *The Global Impact of Religious Violence,* eds. André Gagné, Spyridon Loumakis, and Calogero Miceli, 13-38. Eugene, OR: Wipf and Stock. (Page 129)

Wifall, Walter. "The Sea of Reeds as Sheol." *Zeitschrift für die alttestamentliche Wissenschaft* 92.3 (1980): 325-332. (Page 111)

Wilkinson, Lisa Atwood. 2013. *Socratic Charis: Philosophy Without the Agon.* Lanham, MD: Lexington Books. (Page 143)

Wood, Michael. 2013. *In Search of the First Civilizations.* New York: Random House. (Page 21)

Woodard, Roger D., ed. 2004. *The Cambridge Encyclopedia of the World's Ancient Languages.* Cambridge: Cambridge University Press. (Page 89)

Yadav, Shyam S., David McNeil, and Philip C. Stevenson, eds. 2007. *Lentil: An Ancient Crop for Modern Times.* Dordrecht, Netherlands: Springer Publications. (Page 67)

Zerubavel, Eviatar. 1989. *The Seven Day Circle: The History and Meaning of the Week.* Chicago: University of Chicago Press. (Page 15)

Note on the Illustrations

Tishkoff, Sarah A., and Kenneth K. Kidd. "Implications of Bio-geography of Human Populations for 'Race' and Medicine." *Nature Genetics* 36.11s (2004): S2.

Yudell, Michael, Dorothy Roberts, Rob DeSalle, and Sarah Tishkoff. "Taking Race out of Human Genetics." *Science* 351, no. 6273 (2016): 564-565.

Introduction

Hughes, Jeremy. *Secrets of the Times: Myth and History in Biblical Chronology.* 1990. Vol. 66. London: A&C Black.

Van Seters, John. "Is There Any Historiography in the Hebrew Bible? A Hebrew-Greek Comparison." *Journal of Northwest Semitic Languages* 28.2 (2002): 1-25.

ABOUT THE AUTHOR, ILLUSTRATOR, AND EXPERT

Donna Jo Napoli
is a professor of linguistics and social justice at Swarthmore College, the mother of five, and the grandmother of eight. She has written more than 80 books for children and young adults, including National Geographic's *Treasury of Greek Mythology, Treasury of Egyptian Mythology, Treasury of Norse Mythology,* and *Tales From the Arabian Nights.* While Napoli's undergraduate major was mathematics and her graduate work was in linguistics, she has a profound love of storytelling. Her website is *donnajonapoli.com.*

Christina Balit
is a graduate of the Chelsea School of Art and the Royal College of Art, London. An award-winning dramatist and artist, Christina has illustrated more than 20 published children's books, including *Blodin the Beast, The Planet Gods, The Lion Illustrated Bible for Children,* and National Geographic's *Zoo in the Sky, Treasury of Greek Mythology, Treasury of Egyptian Mythology, Treasury of Norse Mythology,* and *Tales From the Arabian Nights.* Balit is also a published author and playwright.

Helen Plotkin
is the director of the Swarthmore College Center for the Study of Classical Jewish Texts. She teaches courses in biblical Hebrew and in classical Hebrew texts at Swarthmore. She educates adults, teens, and families at Mekom Torah, a Philadelphia-area Jewish community learning project.

INDEX

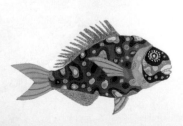

Thanks from my heart and soul to Helen Plotkin. —*Donna Jo Napoli*

For my beautiful, glorious, and loving father, George Michel Balit,
who, before he died earlier this year, watched me paint quite a few of these
illustrations on his kitchen table and contributed all sorts of "helpful"
suggestions along the way. Which was absolutely fine by me as he taught
me how to paint and draw in the first place. —*Christina Balit*

In memory of my mother, Billie Plotkin, who would have loved
Donna Jo and this book. —*Helen Plotkin*

Acknowledgments: My guide in these stories is the Rabbi Helen Plotkin. She met with me regularly from September 2016 through February 2017, and after that, whenever needed, through December 2017 to go over the stories in Hebrew and English, pointing out so many things I never could have known without her. My gratitude to her is unending. She also introduced me to the works of Robert Alter and Everett Fox, which were foundational throughout this book.

Since 1888, the National Geographic Society has funded more than 12,000 research, exploration, and preservation projects around the world. The Society receives funds from National Geographic Partners, LLC, funded in part by your purchase. A portion of the proceeds from this book supports this vital work. To learn more, visit **natgeo.com/info.**

NATIONAL GEOGRAPHIC and Yellow Border Design are trademarks of the National Geographic Society, used under license.

For more information, visit **nationalgeographic.com,** call 1-800-647-5463, or write to the following address:

National Geographic Partners
1145 17th Street N.W.
Washington, D.C. 20036-4688 U.S.A.

Visit us online at nationalgeographic.com/books

For librarians and teachers: ngchildrensbooks.org

More for kids from National Geographic: **natgeokids.com**

National Geographic Kids magazine inspires children to explore their world with fun yet educational articles on animals, science, nature, and more. Using fresh storytelling and amazing photography, *Nat Geo Kids* shows kids ages 6 to 14 the fascinating truth about the world—and why they should care. **kids.nationalgeographic.com/subscribe**

For information about special discounts for bulk purchases, please contact National Geographic Books Special Sales: specialsales@natgeo.com

For rights or permissions inquiries, please contact National Geographic Books Subsidiary Rights: bookrights@natgeo.com

Designed by Callie Broaddus

Hardcover ISBN: 978-1-4263-3538-9
Reinforced library binding ISBN: 978-1-4263-3539-6

Printed in China
19/PPS/1

— Illustrations Credits —

All Illustrations by Christina Balit.

BI=Bridgeman Images; GI=Getty Images; IS=iStockphoto; SS=Shutterstock

15 (LO), Ikon Images/GI; 21 (LO), Corbis Documentary/GI; 25, Kristian Bell/GI; 31 (LO), andipantz/GI; 39 (LO), Larry Knupp/SS; 42, Kennis & Kennis/MSF/Science Photo Library; 49, DeAgostini/GI; 55, Cheryl Lynn Mitchell/GI; 61, Andrea Willmore/SS; 67, Vova Shevchuk/SS; 75, Herlanzer/SS; 83, IS/GI; 89, YaniG/GI; 94, IS/GI; 104 (LO), Viktor Kochetkov/SS; 111, Callie Broaddus, NG Staff; 118 (UP), Javier Cruz Acosta/GI; 124, Peter Popov Cpp/SS; 129, Scene from Beowulf (gouache on paper) by Howat, Andrew (20th Century); Private Collection/BI; 135, Victory stele for King Mesha of Moab at Dibon, Eastern Jordan, 842 BC (basalt) by Phoenician, (9th century BC)/BI; 143, Achilles Defeating Hector, 1630-32 (oil on panel) by Rubens, Peter Paul (1577-1640)/BI; 149, sedmak/IS/GI; 155, Tetra images RF/GI; 161, Reinhard Dirscherl/WaterFrame.de/GI; 169, Job and his friends by English School, (20th century); Private Collection/BI; 173, EyeEm/GI; 179, IS/GI; 180, Lonely Planet Images/GI; 187, Mageda Merbouh/GI; 194 (LE), Philippe Clement/NPL/Minden Pictures; 194 (CTR), MARKA/Alamy; 194 (RT), StockFood/GI; 195 (UP), Dan Breckwoldt/SS; 195 (LO LE), simplytheyu/IS/GI; 195 (LO RT), Oskanov/IS/GI; 196 (UP), youngyut/IS/GI; 196 (CTR), Mimi Ditchie Photography/GI; 196 (LO), Stocktrek Images, Inc./Alamy